A Guide to the Birds of North Andros Island

Joseph T Steensma
Nick Morken
Larry Wiedman
Luanettee Colebrooke

SHEBA Media

St. Louis, Missouri

Sheba Media
12760 Corum Way Drive
St. Louis, Missouri

A Guide to Birds of North Andros Island
Joseph T. Steensma
ISBN 978-0988638204

Dedicated to the people of Andros Island

We would also like to thank Otis Marshall who has been our eyes and ears for so many years. Otis has led us to so many birds over the years that we would be remiss if we did not acknowledge his contributions to this effort. He is a great naturalist, from whom we are always learning.

From Joe:
A special thanks to Andy Pyle and Jason Morrison. Andy has put me on a lot of great birds over the years. He is like a good luck charm and I am always guaranteed to see something rare when I am with him. Jason Morrison is an incredible naturalist who has taught me a great deal about the natural world and (more importantly) life. Lastly, none of this work would be possible without the support of Kristie, who has spent nearly every New Year's Holiday for the past 24 years without her husband, who was out counting birds in a swamp on Andros Island.

CONTENTS

WARNING

Birding is an activity that may be extreme at times, it may be dangerous; but one thing it will always be is FUN. If you are birding and not having fun, you are either doing it wrong or with the wrong people. To help you in your birding career we have a few rules that we feel are pretty important to share.

Rule #1: Don't bird-watch with jerks.

If a person is a jerk when he is not bird-watching, he will very likely be a jerk when he is bird-watching. Bird-watching with jerks is a bit like hunting with former vice president of the United States, Dick Chaney: stuffy at best ... life threatening at worst.

Rule #2: Don't be a know-it-all.

Look, we have all known those people who "know everything" about whatever their passion is. You know the type—the "been-there, done-that" person who is a total buzz kill. Those people fall squarely into the "jerk" category. You DO NOT WANT TO FALL IN THAT CATEGORY (See rule #1)!

Rule #3: Don't be a buzz kill.

We have birded (Note: bird is a verb as well as a noun) on Andros Island hundreds of times and still get jazzed about seeing all types of birds that we have seen thousands of times (though Joe is not a huge fan of Black-faced Grassquits). We hate birding with people who say things like, "Oh, we saw that bird yesterday" or "That bird is boring."

The point is, no bird deserves to be written off as "common" or "just a(n) [fill in the blank]." How would you like it if the birds watching you said, "Oh, it's just another female human," or "It's just another rude American."? That doesn't feel very good, does it? Well, birds have feelings, too. Don't write off a bird just because it isn't super sexy. Maybe it has a cool personality or lives in some pretty terrific place. Maybe it is an amazing singer or has some crazy behaviors. Just remember you are an individual, and so is each of the birds you will be looking at. Nobody, including birds, likes hanging out with judgmental people.

Rule #4: Everything is a game.

For us, birding is not just some leisure activity; it is a chance for adventure, competition, and amazing shared experiences. We strongly encourage you to create small challenges or games while birding.

We have what we call "beer birds." A list of beer birds is established before the spotting begins. Usually (at least for us), the list contains birds we really want to see or one that is special to us for some reason (e.g., it rescued us from a burning building when we were infants). When someone spots a beer bird, the rest of the team buys that person a beer later in the evening.

If you are with a group that happens to be under twenty-one or eighteen, depending on the law of the host country, you can make a "candy birds" list. Whatever it may be, challenge and competition make birding more fun.

Also, if you are not too fond of the name of any bird, go ahead and give it a new name. We have dubbed the Painted Bunting "P-Bizzle," not because we dislike the name "Painted Bunting" but because we felt it was too much of a bad-ass not to have a nickname. We also write songs about birds we see (Many of these are "R-rated" songs and, given our professions and standing in society, we don't feel it would be a good career move to release our album just yet). These are all things that add to the excitement of a bird venture.

Rule #5: Don't bird-watch naked.

This is the voice of experience. It sounds like a fantastic idea, but trust us on this one: IT IS NOT! The list of reasons this is not a good idea is pretty long, but it can be summed up in four words: bugs, burns, thorns, and chaffing.

Rule #6: Respect ... everything.

You might have surmised that Nick and Joe are always up to a party while bird-watching. We honestly believe that bird-watching is a celebration of creation. But just because we have a blast every time we bird, doesn't mean we are disrespectful. Quite the contrary, we deeply respect the property, people, and creatures (of all types) we encounter while we are birding.

The people of Andros Island are amazingly kind and friendly, but don't be a jerk and go onto property to watch birds without permission. The birds of the island are awesome, but don't plow through a patch of orchids (ignoring their beauty and disrespecting their lives) to see a bird.

The point: Respect the dignity of all people, places, and creatures while you are having a ball bird-watching.

Rule #7: Share the love.

You may have figured this out already; we are on a mission, and we need your help. Our mission is to spread the Gospel of Birds. If you are coming to Andros to bird-watch, you probably have a few extra bucks, so pack an extra set of binoculars to leave at the school or an extra field guide (maybe even this one!) to give to a kid you meet. Encourage people to look through your spotting scope or go birding with you.

We believe that the more people who see the amazing diversity and complete awesomeness of the bird life on Andros, the more likely that this special place will be protected.

ORGANIZATION AND STRUCTURE

This is not an identification guide. The purpose of this guide is to help the user find birds on the island and the habitats that are ideal for certain species of birds. This guide is intended for use as a companion guide to any book on birds of the West Indies you can get your hands on.

That said, we use (and *highly recommend*) *Birds of the West Indies,* the field guide by Raphael et al., published by Princeton University Press. The references in this book will coincide with *Birds of the West Indies*. We list the plate number next to each species where the image of this bird can be seen in Raphael's book. *Birds of the West Indies* will help with identifying each species, while the book you are now reading will help narrow down the species you are most likely to see on North Andros and where to find them.

This book describes the best places to find approximately 150 of the most common and/or most interesting birds found on the island. *The text intentionally focuses on wintering species, as opposed to migrants that simply pass through on their way to other places.* The reason for this is that these transient birds can be hit and miss and are not nearly as reliable as the birds that winter or live on North Andros year-round.

This book is not intended to provide a comprehensive listing of every bird one could possibly see on the island. It is also not exhaustive in terms of the habitats included in the text. In fact, there are hundreds of specific locations for which we have written detailed species records, but they are not all included in this book. We are not trying to cheat the reader and save all of the best spots for ourselves (though the thought did cross our minds). Rather, we want to focus on the most productive birding locations on the island so that, if you are new to Andros, you can have a great birding experience on your first trip.

We have found many of these spots through years of exploration. While we hope this guide gives you a distinct advantage in your bird-watching adventures on North Andros, we also encourage everyone to explore the island and find your own "secret hotspots," just as we have done through the years.

MAP

One of the main goals of this guide is to get you to see the birds you want to see. The following map highlights some of the key birding areas we will reference in the book. Some birds can be seen throughout the island. For the more rare or hard-to-spot species, we indicate which area on the island will give you the best chance of scoring a goal bird.

1. Red Bays
2. Jungle Pond
3. Joulter Cays
4. Lowe Sound
5. Money Point
6. Morgan's Bluff
7. Nicholls Town
8. Conch Sound
9. Mastic Point
10. San Andros Airport
11. Mennonite Farm
12. Bahamas Agricultural & Marine Research Institute
13. London Creek
14. Owens Town
15. Stafford Creek
16. Blanket Sound (Forfar Field Station)
17. Gobi Lake
18. Staniard Creek
19. Small Hope Bay
20. Calabash Bay
21. Fresh Creek
22. Blue Holes National Park
23. Twin Lakes
24. Tarpon Pond
25. AUTEC
26. Cargill Creek
27. Behring Point
28. West Side National Park

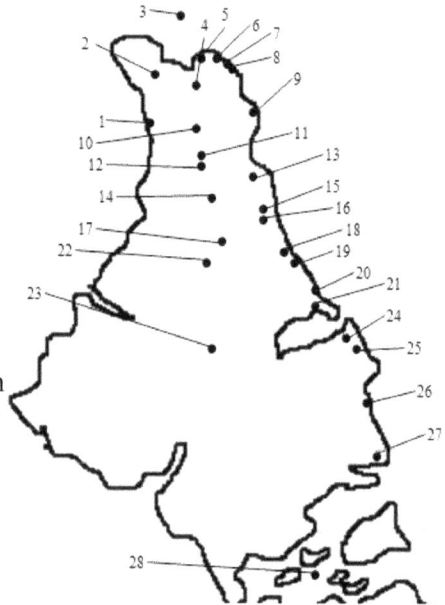

INTRODUCTION

Bird-watching is a hobby attracting millions of new enthusiastic birders each year. Some enjoy watching the avifauna from the safety of their back porches. Others prefer a more extreme side of the activity, going on adventures that span the globe. No matter your intent as a birder, the use of a field guide is essential in areas that are new or unfamiliar to you. In fact, we always carry a few different identification guides with us, even when we are on Andros Island.

There are several types of field guides for different regions of the globe. This guide was created specifically for North Andros Island, Bahamas. Even more specific than that, we focused on the most common wintering birds of Andros Island. This guide will help you not only identify the species you see but also organize where and when the bird was spotted. The purpose of this guide is to help birders plan trips in order to maximize your bird-watching time.

Review the following features before getting started:

Ratings

Each species listed in this guide has an individual rating. Honestly, these ratings are actually somewhat arbitrary. However, we mean well. A common complaint we have about most field guides is that they don't indicate the relative abundance of a particular bird in a specific area. There are also some birds (e.g., the Red-Legged Thrush) that could use some better publication, because the field guides never do them justice in terms of how cool or beautiful they are. We also think that there are some birds (e.g., the Reddish Egret) that have really cool behaviors, and if people know about those behaviors, they may hang out a bit longer just to see this bird do its "thing." It is with this in mind that we created our categories.

Along with each bird description, you will find ratings for Wow-Factor, Behavior, and Rarity. Each of these ratings is based on a 5-point scale. If a bird has fives across the board, this is a dream bird that is really rare, really beautiful, and has some pretty cool behaviors. On the other hand, do not discount those species whose ratings might not be the highest; every bird is special in its own right.

Wow-Factor	Rarity	Behavior
🪶 🪶 🪶 🪶 🪶	🪶 🪶 🪶 🪶 🪶	🪶 🪶 🪶 🪶 🪶

Wow-Factor: A "five out of five" in this category would indicate a species of vibrant color or strikingly contrasted plumage. You will definitely have a "bird-gasm" if you see a bird with a five in this category. If you are wondering if you have ever had a bird-gasm, you haven't; if you had one you would know.

Behavior: A "five out of five" in this category would include birds with such unique behaviors that they are memorable if only for that reason. An example is the Reddish Egret's unique dancing skills!

Rarity: A "five out of five" in this category would represent a species that is quite uncommon, not only to this region but in general, such as a Kirtland's Warbler or Greater Flamingo. This category is a lot less subjective. Scores are based on twenty-four years of observational data collected during the winter and spring. It is important to note, however, that some birds that are fairly abundant on North Andros (e.g., Great Lizard Cuckoo) are actually not very common elsewhere. In other words, some birds could be quite rare globally but only receive a 2 or 3 because of their abundance on North Andros.

Most of the species found in this guide are migratory, so you may be able to spot them in parts of North America, as well. The "Notes" space allows you to jot down a few thoughts for this species. We encourage you to create nicknames for different birds or log your memorable accounts with different individual birds.

TOP 10 LIST

This feature allows you to list your top ten goal birds for this region. A goal bird is one that you want to see more than others. Make sure you use this list to rank your goal birds and go the distance to reach your goal!

Species	Location(s)

CHAPTER ONE

A PRIMER ON ANDROS ISLAND

Andros Island was "discovered" by Columbus in 1492 during his first voyage to the new world, although Lucayan and Arawak Indians lived on the island for centuries before then. Columbus named the island La Isle del Espiritu Santo, or "Isle of the Holy Spirit." By the mid 1700s, most maps referred to it as "Andros" for the Colonial Governor of New England, Sir Edmund Andros. Many Bahamians today, however, claim the name comes from the Aegean Isle of Andros.

Andros Island, approximately 115 by 40 miles, is the largest of the Bahamian Islands and the fifth largest in the Caribbean area. Compared to the other Bahamian Islands, Andros is relatively unpopulated with about 8,500 people. For the most part, they live near the east coast. Since Bahamian independence, Andros has had a declining population from a high of over twelve thousand.

The majority of people rely on the sea for their livelihood. The pace of life is slow, and the days on Andros are not geared to the clock. The Bahamians on Andros are very friendly and are, for the most part, eager to assist and answer any questions about their home island.

There are five distinct vegetation zones in the Andros subtropical biome. These zones include the once extensive forest of termite-resistant Caribbean pine, savannah, coppice, swash, and mangrove.

The terrestrial fauna includes numerous species of invertebrates, reptiles, and birds of interest to biologists.

The extensive coral reef, just one of the many marine habitats, lies between a few hundred yards and one-and-a-half miles off the east coast. It is the third-largest barrier reef in the world and is considered by many to be one of the most diverse and pristine reefs in the world. The coral, fish, and other marine organisms in the clear, shallow water inside and around the reef are abundant and easily seen by snorkelers and SCUBA divers.

Just beyond the reef, the continental shelf drops 2,500 meters into the Tongue of the Ocean (TOTO). This drop constitutes the feature known as "The Wall" in diving circles and local folklore. Several caves, the coral reef, oolite shoals off the north coast, lime muds on the west coast, and the blue holes (both inland and oceanic) are of geological interest and have had significant influence on the island's economic and cultural development.

Some of the blue holes contain both fresh and salt water. Jacques Cousteau's book, *Three Adventures*, and *National Geographic,* September 1970, are readily available references with good pictures and descriptions of Andros and the blue holes.

It is our steadfast recommendation that if you visit Andros Island, you should take some snorkeling gear along with your binoculars. With access to the third-largest barrier reef, marine and fresh water blue holes, patch reefs, and tidal creeks, you are bound to find some amazing sea creatures to go with the breathtaking terrestrial wildlife. Couple that with some of the best fishing in the hemisphere, and you have a nature lover's paradise!

Now, don't get us wrong: We still believe birds steal the show on North Andros, but the reefs and blue holes definitely deserve a visit or two. We also occasionally see tropicbirds and shearwaters when we snorkel, so if you are a hard-core birder, you could easily justify a trip to the reef where you might see some good pelagic species! In fact, we often see the best pelagic species on fishing trips to TOTO. We consider such birding/fishing trips our version of multitasking. If you would like to multitask in the same way, we recommend you talk to Ricardo or Franklin Riley in South Blanket Sound (they can be reached at Forfar Field Station) or Prescott Smith at Stafford Creek Lodge.

CLIMATE

Temperatures on Andros are moderate year round. The single most important climatic agent affecting them is the warm trade wind. During the winter months, the Gulf Stream warms the islands; then in May, southerly trade winds return to gently cool them.

The windy months of August, September, and October have the greatest risk of tropical storms or hurricanes.

Temperatures range in the eighties to nineties during the day and 68° to 75°F in the evening.

The winter months of November, December, January, and February, which can be cooler, have daytime temperatures in the 70° to 80° range. Nighttime temperatures can dip into the low forties.

The spring months of March, April, and May can be dry and not as windy. Temperatures average in the seventies with night temperatures in the sixties to seventies.

June, July, and August, the summer months, can be extremely hot, with temperatures well over 90°F. Moderate to light winds keep the average temperatures between 70° to 95°F.

The average monthly rainfall is given in Figure 2.1.

To be clear, we feel the best time to visit Andros (at least for bird-watching) is during the winter months, although the weather in the winter can be highly variable. We recall one particularly cold spell in 2002, when the high temperature did not get above 60° for two weeks, and nighttime temperatures were just damn cold! This is highly unusual, but it can happen. It is important to pack long pants, a warm sweater or two, a windbreaker, and a hat.

Also, the subtropical sun can be intense even on a cool day, so bring sunscreen. We could go on and on about preparing for every type of weather scenario, but if you are going to Andros to bird-watch, you are probably not a rookie. Come prepared for everything.

Figure 2.1: Average monthly rainfall (cm.) on Andros Island.

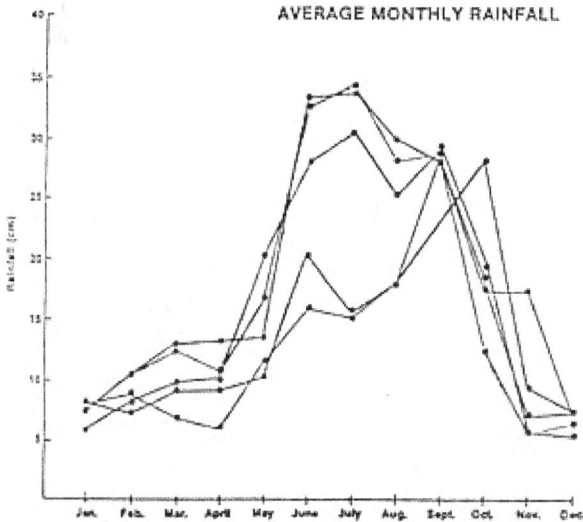

AVERAGE MONTHLY RAINFALL

THINGS THAT BURN, ITCH, STING, SLITHER, OR ARE OTHERWISE NOT NICE

Andros is in a part of the world where there are critters that bite, sting, itch, or otherwise pester humans. *The reality is that the degree of this pestering is not nearly as bad as other parts of the tropics or even the United States,* for that matter. For example, the mosquitoes and biting flies in the northern United States in July are a million times worse (this is merely an estimate) than what you are likely to experience on Andros. Still, there are creatures to approach with care, and it is prudent to plan and pack accordingly.

The Sand Flea

Let's start with the worst critter first. We have found over the years that we (specifically two of the authors of this text, Joe and Nick) seem to be very tasty to sand fleas. If we were being perfectly honest, we would tell you that sand fleas are the spawn of the devil and were sent from hell to pester us. Some people (like Doc Wiedman, another contributor to this text) seem to be immune to the evil that is the sand flea (which makes us distrust Doc, just a little bit).

Sand fleas, as their name implies, hang out in sand, on the lookout for exposed human flesh, where they suck their blood meal from the unsuspecting victim. If that were not bad enough, some people (e.g., Joe and Nick) are more allergic to the flea bites than other people. These critters can cause itchiness, which is why we highly recommend packing hydrocortisone or Benadryl cream (or both). In fact, pack that stuff no matter where you go.

How does one avoid these satanic gargoyles? Well, you don't. All you can do is wear long pants and maybe bug spray, though we have found bug spray has only a modest effect on these little evil doers. Doc Wiedman swears by garlic. His prescription is to start taking garlic pills two weeks before your trip and continuing through the trip. This has worked for many of our students over the years, but the effect was not as pronounced for Joe and Nick.

Also, these little devils are not very good flyers, so any amount of wind will suppress them. Don't be fooled, however. On the beach, there is often a nice breeze; but just off the beach, the wind may die down. They will be waiting.

The bottom line with these critters is that they are: (1) evil, (2) selective in their prey (apparently favoring handsome guys like Joe and Nick), (3) itch inducing, and (4) *a tiny price to pay for seeing awesome birds.*

After the sand flea, all other beasts and nuisances pale in comparison. Let's take them in order.

Millipede

Is there a giant biting millipede on Andros Island? Yes. Does it hurt when it bites? Uh, yes. Will you get over it? Yes, you will.

Seriously though, *the only way you even see these critters is when you go looking for them.* You have to turn over logs and dig around to find these dudes. They are pretty amazing and neat to see, but avoid petting them. Our advice is DON'T TOUCH GIANT MILLIPEDES.

The Sand Scorpion

Here is the deal with this little guy: Doc Wiedman has been doing research on Andros for thirty-five years, Joe Steensma for twenty-four years, and Nick Morken for ten years…and we have seen this scorpion fewer than five times combined! It is rare, but it can sting (and it would suck if you got stung).

It hangs out in shoes and towels you might leave on the floor. Our advice: ALWAYS CHECK YOUR SHOES, and shake them out before you put them on. Hang your towels, and don't leave clothes on the floor (now we feel like your mother: "Clean your room!").

Mosquitoes

Mosquitoes are actually not bad in most areas. In the winter they are rarely a problem except near fresh water and at dusk. Our advice: Bug spray works great for these guys. Get the stuff with DEET. If you are one of those people who are "anti-DEET," we respect your opinion, but suck it up! A few days of DEET are not that big of a deal. Plus, Joe is an environmental toxicologist, and he uses it. So how bad can it be, really?

Doctor Flies

Doctor flies are more of a spring and summer problem. What makes them a problem is that they bite, and it hurts. This is just another reason to go birding during winter and early spring: better birds and no doctor flies.

One remedy that seems to repulse these creatures is sunscreen. We apply a thick layer of sunscreen and never seem to get bitten. Our advice: Go birding in the winter, or apply lots of sunscreen.

Black Widow

The black widow is a reclusive spider that would prefer not to see you. The male black widow is tiny and basically lives in fear, knowing that the end is near for him. It has a sad and lonely life (like Nick before he started birdwatching). Once he mates with his selected bride, she eats him. So, it is the female you really have to watch for. Actually, both are venomous, but the female has a much more potent venom. Both can elicit a profound allergic response, as well, so we always carry an EpiPen with us when we have students, just to be on the safe side.

Our advice: Check clothing before getting dressed, and don't stick your hand (or any part of your body) into a dark hole. Spiders live in such places and might bite you if you invade their home.

Snakes

All snakes on the island are non-venomous, so you have no reason to be afraid of the snakes on North Andros, unless of course you are ophidiophobic (have a phobia of snakes). The most common snake is a type of constrictor called the Bahama Boa. It is a stunningly beautiful snake that eats mice and rats *and people*. OK, that was uncalled for; it really does not eat people. In fact, it is a shy snake that is far more active at night. These snakes are perfectly harmless, and you should consider yourself lucky to see one. Our advice: If you see one, take a picture.

Poisonwood

As the name implies, poisonwood is not a critter. It is a plant. Actually, it is a woody plant that can grow into a tree.

As in every area in the world, there are some plants to which some people are allergic. The Bahamas are no exception. Some people are not affected by poisonwood, whereas others have severe allergic reactions.

Poisonwood is a tree with a smooth but patchy bark. In fact, the bark itself looks like the tree could be having an allergic reaction. If you see a tree that fits this description it is likely poisonwood.

Poisonwood has a very distinctive leaf—a green oval with a bright yellow vein down the center.

Our advice: AS SOON AS YOU GET TO ANDROS ASK SOMEONE TO POINT OUT POISONWOOD. From then on, do not touch it. If you do touch it, wash your hands (or affected area) immediately. Also, long pants and long-sleeved shirts help prevent direct dermal contact with the bush.

Sawgrass/Cutgrass/Smilax

By any name this plant is wicked. It won't cause an allergic reaction, but it will cut you. Think of a long paper cut across your shin. Now think of that a couple dozen times. Sawgrass is very common in bracken fern, savannah, and grassland environments.

Owens Town (a great birding hotspot to be discussed later) is loaded with the stuff. If you walk through the grass at Owens Town in shorts and/or sandals, expect those little cuts. Our advice: Wear long pants and closed-toed shoes.

Of course, there could be other things that make you itch or that sting, but those listed above are the most common or dangerous. *It is important to remember that, while there are a few insects or plants that warrant caution, the same could be said anywhere in the world.* As we stated earlier, but want to repeat, the authors feel that there are far fewer nuisances on North Andros than in many other great birding locations.

The most important thing to remember is that if you are going into the bush, wear long pants, hiking shoes or boots, sunscreen, and bug spray. And pack some antihistamine and steroid creams, just in case.

CULTURE

The Bahamian, or more specifically, Androsian culture is not easy to explain. It is a conglomerate of many different cultures. With the British influence on language and government, African ancestry on its population, Caribbean influence on its day-to-day lifestyle and religion, and relationship to the United States economically, the island is a true amalgamation of cultures.

This is not to say the people of Andros do not have their own culture. Far from it! We merely call your attention to the diversity that informs the Androsian culture and that while it has some elements that seem similar to "Western" culture, it also has others that are vastly different.

Generally speaking, the people on Andros are extremely generous but might appear a little reserved compared to other places the United States, Canada, or Europe. Faith is extremely important to many Androsians, and the church forms part of the nexus of social life on the island. Whatever your own religious beliefs, we highly recommend that you attend a church service if you can afford the time.

Androsians are very accepting of other people and are often interested in learning from people who might have different perspectives from their own. We have always made it a point to engage with people as we are out bird-watching. We have learned more about the history and culture of Andros by walking through the bush or grabbing a cold Kalik (a high quality local beer) with the locals at the end of a long day of birding than we ever have reading a book.

The people on Andros are generous, peaceful, and very friendly unless you are playing dominos. Things can get a little crazy playing dominos! The most important point to remember if you are from the USA is that THIS IS NOT THE USA! Respect the culture and people who live here. Respect their property, their faith, and their way of life. Get to know the people as well as you get to know the birds. When you do, you will find that they are equally beautiful, fascinating, and enchanting.

FOOD AND LODGING

The first thing to keep in mind is that Andros is a "family island," meaning that it is more rural. There are not (thank God!) mega-hotels with casinos and waterslides. Even the swankiest place on the island seems very simple. The purpose of birding on North Andros is to unplug and get away from the hustle and bustle. If you are the type who gets uncomfortable easily or needs the sound of cars outside your door or airplanes taking off in the middle of the night, Andros may not be for you. If, however, you are willing to give up some "creature comforts" in order to hear the waves lapping the beach while you fall into a dream in which a flock of Painted Buntings carry you away to an Androsian thicket and show you how they become so colorful—a recurring dream for Joe—then, you are in luck.

There are a few places to stay while on North Andros; each one of them has its own unique charms and serves a particular niche. While we have our favorite places to stay, you might have different tastes and needs. The descriptions below are not intended to serve as recommendations. Rather, we hope that they offer a description of what you can expect when you visit.

Love at First Sight (Sheila's): Stafford Creek

Sheila is the proprietor of this amazing property, which is nestled along Stafford Creek on Blanket Sound. Sheila may be the best chef ever in the history of the world. The view is awesome, and the food is better than the view. Its central location makes it ideal for the birder who wants to hit a lot of spots in a short amount of time. The pool is a big hit with kids, if you are traveling with fledglings.

Small Hope Bay Lodge

Small Hope Bay Lodge is a beautiful property on the beach. This all-inclusive resort offers many extras including snorkeling, scuba, fishing, birding trips, and more. While it is close to some prime birding spots (Calabash, Fresh Creek, and Blue Holes National Park), it is not as central as Shelia's. It is, however, still in a prime location. The staff is extraordinarily friendly and very helpful. There is also a well-maintained nature trail on site.

Kamalame Cay

Kamalame Cay is a high end resort just to the east of Staniard Creek. As you might expect, it is beautiful and probably has the most creature comforts of all the places on the island. Fishing, snorkeling, scuba, sailing, birding, and a host of other activities are available. The food is excellent. This might be on the pricey side for many travelers, but it has an excellent reputation and could be a fit for those who want a little more post-birding pampering.

Forfar Field Station

Forfar is on Blanket Sound, which is one of the most beautiful beaches in the Bahamas. It is a field station or educational and ecotourism facility that offers amazing educational adventures for people of all ages. Guests can snorkel, bird-watch, scuba dive, sail, windsurf, and so much more. We have stayed at Forfar countless times and love it. That said, it is a bit on the rustic side and definitely geared more for the adventure traveler who has little need to be indulged. The food is great, but the view and the learning are exceptional.

THE IMPORTANCE OF ANDROS

From a birder's perspective, Andros Island is a very special place. It is within one hundred fifty miles from the US mainland. It is by far the largest island in the Bahamas and the fifth-largest island in the Caribbean. It boasts a variety of habitats that is unmatched anywhere else in the Bahaman archipelago. While these attributes make it a highly desirable place to bird-watch, none of them is the main reason Andros is so special.

What makes Andros unique is that it is relatively unstudied, and we believe there are many important discoveries yet to be made on the island. Certainly, there have been many people who have studied the birds of this island (Rick Perkins, Mike Balz, Rivean Riley, and Otis Marshall are a few who come to mind), but it is unlikely that any of those naturalists would be so bold as to suggest that they fully understand the avian ecology of Andros. In fact, after more than twenty years of chasing birds on North Andros, we still find her difficult to understand. She is complicated and constantly changing.

It is this dynamism that keeps us coming back, season after season, year after year. For example, take the case of the Yellow-rumped Warbler. In the early 1990s, we could go days in the peak of the winter season without seeing a single bird. Spring forward to the turn of the century, and we would find dozens of Yellow-rumpeds in a single tree! What changed? The introduction and proliferation of Brazilian Pepper provided a reliable food source upon which the Yellow-rumpeds gorged, and in so doing, they continued to spread the seeds of the Brazilian Pepper until it could be found on every corner of North Andros Island. The Brazilian Pepper population seems to have stabilized, and so has the number of wintering Yellow-rumped Warblers. This stabilization has occurred at the same time we were observing consequential changes in other wintering bird populations on the island.

Certainly, there are a number of external factors that can affect these fluctuations (e.g., West Nile virus decimated some songbird populations), but there are also a number of factors that are internal to the island. We believe these have had a positive impact on wintering bird populations on Andros Island and why Andros will continue to grow in importance as wintering grounds for migratory birds.

There is no question that Andros Island is, and has been, absolutely essential to the survival of many species of birds. For thousands of years, birds migrating south from the continental United States have come to Andros to find a large island ecosystem with everything they needed to fatten up for a long journey north a few months later.

We hypothesize that everything was perfect until *Homo sapiens* came along. Actually, *Homo sapiens* did not really do massive damage to the ecology of Andros until the introduction of the sub-species human known as *Homo sapiens capitalistic pigus* (otherwise known as the "Capitalist Pig" variety of human beings). This particular sub-species of human looked upon this vast island ecosystem and saw piles of money, rather than one of the most important wintering grounds in the world for migratory birds.

You see, Andros, a very large and sparsely populated island, had the misfortune of growing some highly desirable and easily accessible timber. Logging was easy on this large, flat island—too easy. Within a short time, starting in the 1950s and culminating in the late 1970s, one company scalped the island. Old-growth pine and coppice environments were decimated; and the migratory birds that, for generations, had relied upon Andros as a place to fatten up for the winter, arrived each year to find an increasingly deforested shell of the island.

When we started studying the birds on Andros, logging had stopped a mere fifteen years prior. The island had not fully recovered (it still hasn't), and there were still many vast, open fields where forest once stood and would someday stand again.

Over the past twenty-five years, we have observed the growth in wintering populations of shore birds (such as Piping Plovers), songbirds (such as Swainson's Warblers), and pelagic species. We have also seen evidence of increasing populations of year-round residents, including the threatened Bahama Swallow, Reddish Egret, and Bahama Yellowthroat.

At the same time, however, we have witnessed decreases in wintering populations of hawks of all sorts, most notably the Red-tailed Hawk and the Northern Harrier, as well as other species. While others might take a glass-half-empty approach to these population declines, we believe these changes in populations are a result of Andros itself changing. It is changing back to what is once was—a great forest with two dominant woodland communities: coppice and Caribbean pine. This is thanks to two factors that cannot be overstated.

While there is no question that the cessation of logging has helped restore the ecological balance on Andros, without the Bahamas National Trust and the efforts of Eric Cary (and countless others), some of the most precious areas of Andros would remain vulnerable. The establishment of the West Side and Blue Holes National Park on Andros placed some of the most valuable ecosystems in the hemisphere in preserves forever. These actions, coupled with the realization among many in the birding community that Andros is a crown jewel among North American birding locations, gives us great hope that the future is bright for Andros and the birds that rely upon this unique place.

CHAPTER TWO

VEGETATIVE ZONES

A NOTE ABOUT BOTANISTS

If birders are considered to be "geeks" or "nerds," what are plant lovers? Super-nerds? Mega-geeks? Don't get us wrong. We appreciate plant-nerds (mostly because they make birders look pretty cool, in comparison), but honestly, what kind of challenge is it to identify a plant? THEY DON'T EVEN MOVE! You can spend all day studying a plant, and it will never fly away. You can be very, very lazy and still be an exceptional botanist, but if you want to be an awesome birder you have to hustle. We are not saying this to be unkind, but if the truth hurts, then all we can do is apologize for our honesty.

Now that we have established the superiority of birders over botanists, you might ask why we would have a whole chapter devoted to plants. Well, we have found that birds like plants. If birds like plants, then *we* like plants. Therefore, as an extension of that rationale, we like botanists. You see, understanding plants and plant communities is really just a means to an end. For us, the goal is always to see more birds. As much as it pains us to admit it, going birding with a botanist can be very helpful (if you can tolerate them stopping every ten steps to check out a plant that will BE IN THE EXACT SAME LOCATION TOMORROW). In case you cannot fit a botanist in your suitcase, we thought we would give you some of what we have learned about the plants of North Andros and some typical birds associated with these plant communities.

VEGITATIVE ZONES

There are five distinct vegetation zones in the Andros subtropical biome. These zones include the once extensive forest of termite-resistant Caribbean pine, savannah, coppice, swash, and mangrove.

In 1979, D.S. Correll recognized nine major community types within these five zones. They are described below and are still used today. He found that the division of the communities is not always clear. These areas where communities mix can be exceptional for birding.

We have included a tenth community in this text: the cultivated garden plot. Many of the common trees and flowers that you will be able to observe on North Andros Island are listed on the following pages.

COASTAL ROCK COMMUNITY

Flora and fauna of the Coastal Rock community can all be characterized by one distinguishing feature: It survives under extreme conditions of exposure. This community receives the full force of the sun, including that reflected from the ocean, and is routinely subjected to salt spray and wave action. The development of plant root systems is limited to tiny pockets of soil found in cracks and deep holes.

Flora adaptations to this niche commonly include:

- Small plant size
- Development of thick, waxy cuticles to limit the rate of evapotranspiration. Some species have developed a covering of short hairs designed to hold a layer of moist air near the leaf's surface.
- The leaves are commonly thick and narrow to reduce the exposed surface area of the plant and further reduce the area available for evapotranspiration.

Typical Flora includes: Seven-year apple, wild thyme, frangiponi, prickly pear, sea ox-eye, and endolithic algae.

Example Locations: Windward Side, Pigeon Cay, Morgan's Bluff.

Birds: This is not a particularly diverse environment in terms of bird life. Shorebirds (e.g., American Oystercatcher, Wilson's Plover, Black Bellied Plovers, Ruddy Turnstone), gulls (Laughing), terns, and night herons are all commonly found in this community. Pelagic species and the Brown Pelican can be seen in flight, but rarely *directly* in this community.

SEA STRAND AND SEA OATS COMMUNITY

The Sea Strand and Sea Oats communities are often seen above or slightly inland from the Coastal Rock community. The flora adaptations of plants living here show some of the same adaptations as the Coastal Rock community to salt as well as:

- Shallow spreading root systems, often with running vines, which help stabilize the sand against wind and waves.

Typical Flora includes: Big lavender, bay cedar, sea oats inkberry, sea lily, purple seaside, sandspur, railroad vine or goat's foot morning glory, sea purslane, sea grape, West Indian almond, *coconut, and *Australian pine.

*Coconut and *Australian pine are not native to the Bahamas. Coconut was probably introduced by nuts drifting on ocean currents; Australian pine was introduced by man.

Example Locations: Staniard Creek Beach, Somerset Beach, and Coconut Grove Beach.

Birds: Again, this environment is not particularly diverse in terms of bird life, but the presence of Australian pine and coconut trees can make a difference in what you see. In some areas, near Tarpon Pond, for example, this community is directly adjacent to a fresh-water or brackish lagoon or pond. In such instances the birding can be quite good.

COASTAL COPPICE COMMUNITY

This community often lies in more protected areas of the beach where sand has accumulated. Plants grow in the sand or a mix of sand and rock.

Floral adaptations include:

- many bright flowers to attract pollinators and tasty fruits that are dispersed by birds.

Typical Flora includes: Anaconda or geiger tree, joewood, wild sage, wild pumpkin, gray nicker, ram's horn, wild dilly, and cocoplum.

Example Locations: Schoolhouse at Blanket Sound Campsite, highway from Forfar Field Station to Stafford Creek Bridge, pass through Coastal Coppice, and Pigeon and Saddleback Keys.

Birds: Considerably more diverse than Sea Strand and Coastal Rock communities, one can expect to see Zenaida Doves, Clapper Rail (both at the schoolhouse and on Pigeon Cay), Thick-billed Vireo, and warblers (Palm is very common).

WHITELAND COMMUNITY

All plants in Whiteland community grow on white sandy soil and may also be found in other communities. Usually, the Whiteland community lies behind or inland from the Coastal Rock and Coppice communities.

Typical Flora includes: Cabbage palm, shoe string fire - epiphyte in tops of cabbage palm, serpent fern (grows among old leaf bases of cabbage palm), milkberry, cinnecord (parts of the plant are used in bush medicine. White flesh around seeds is edible).

Example Locations: Sobal Palm Grove along the Red Bays Road

Birds: Birds in this community can be highly variable, but you are certain to see passerines of interest. We have found that many of the birds that prefer to forage low to the ground

(Bahama and Common Yellowthroat, Palm Warblers, and Black-Faced Grassquits) can be found here.

This community is often a transition community, meaning it may be "sandwiched" between two other plant communities in close proximity. In such cases, a phenomenon called the "edge effect" takes place. This is a phenomenon where the biodiversity (here we are talking about birds) is greater at the edge of the adjoining communities than what would be expected if you were to add the unique species together from each community. From a birder's perspective, this is what we look for: Whiteland community adjacent to two other types of plant communities.

FRESH WATER COMMUNITY

The Fresh Water community is unique to Andros within the Bahamas (other large Caribbean islands like Cuba have examples on them). To have this community present, an island must be large enough to accumulate quantities of fresh water at or near the surface. In some areas the fresh water wicks up through the soil via capillary action in large amounts and is readily available to the vegetation. Sometimes, usually in the spring or fall, after large storms, these communities may even be under water.

Typical Flora includes: Silvertop palm, wild flax, pond apple, sawgrass, cat tail, and grass pink (orchid).

Example Locations: Gobi Lake, Calabash Pond, roadside Ponds from near Mastic Point, low interior areas, the edge of ponds, blue holes, and areas that flood periodically.

Birds: This community is A-M-A-Z-I-N-G for birds. This is where one can see ducks of all sorts, American Bitterns, Least and Pied-billed Grebes, herons of every kind, Solitary and Spotted Sandpipers, Belted Kingfishers, and a wide array of songbirds.

TIDAL FLATS COMMUNITY

The Tidal Flats community comprises flora that can survive occasional flooding by salt water. Normally these areas are very low relief and only inches above sea level at low tide. They are most often found on the leeward side of islands. As one might guess, because of the stark shifts in the system, relatively few plants thrive in this area.

Typical Flora includes: Saltwort, glasswort (small caterpillar on this plant will develop into the world's smallest species of butterfly).
Trees: *Rhizophora mangle, Avicennia nitida,* and *Casuarina equisetifolia.*
Algae: *Scytonema sp.* and *Schizathrix calcicola,* Foraminifera: *Peneroplis sp.*
Example Locations: Staniard Flats, Coastline at Red Bay and area east of road at Love Hill.
Birds: Wading Birds and shorebirds abound in this plant community.

MANGROVE COMMUNITY

The Mangrove community is the most important to the island's stabilization and accretion. It is important, too, for the life that is supported within it. This community surrounds protected bays and along the leeward side of the islands.

Typical flora includes:

- **Red mangrove**: Have long prop (stilt) roots in saltwater. Seeds sprout while still on the tree to form seedlings that drop from the tree and float upright until they touch a muddy bottom and send down roots. Generally small, though largest can grow up to forty feet. Bark is leathery red-brown to prevent loss of water by evaporation. Leaves are shiny yellow-green to dark green. High saline tolerance. Excretes salt through leaves.
- **Black mangrove**: Grows in deeper water than red mangrove. Have long lateral roots (pneumataphores) with short vertical roots (rhizomes) sticking out of the sand to aerate the roots; the roots also acts as a detritus trap. As the detritus deteriorates, the nutrients are absorbed by the roots. Leaves are often covered with salt crystals. Grows up to 25 feet. Bark is dark gray to brown. Leaves are long, firm, and smooth with shiny, dark green on top and downy gray-green underneath. The underside of the leaf may often appear white as a result of excretion of salt by the mangrove. Thick cuticle and bark on stems. Moderately high salt tolerance.
- **White mangrove**: Very stubby pneumatophores; thick, shiny leaves that have a pair of swollen glands near the base that excrete salt. Grows on the beach inland from red and black mangrove.

Grows larger than red to over 40 feet. Bark is dark brown, thick, and furrowed. Leaves are firm and smooth, shiny on both sides and bright green. Thick cuticle. Moderate salt tolerance.

- **Button mangrove**: Only mangrove variety with alternate leaves; all others have opposing leaves. Low salt tolerance. This is found at Forfar near the campfire ring (south of the swing support).
- **Other plants**: Buttonwood has 3-foot twisted branches; leaves are hairy and soft. Fruits look like buttons.

Example Locations: West side of Andros, Stafford Creek, behind Blanket Sound Campsite.

Birds: Ducks, Rails, Thick-billed Vireo, Yellow Warbler, and American Redstart are common, as are a number of songbirds.

BLACKLAND COMMUNITY

The Blackland community is often subdivided into two sub-units: *high coppice and low coppice.* It contains broad leaf plants and a higher diversity of plants than any other community. The trees provide protection from sun for ferns and orchids (*Bromelides*) anchored on trunks, which can grow in abundance. This community forms in the richest and best-developed soil in Bahamas.

Typical Flora includes: Bakam apple, orchids, mahogany, wild fig, pusin wood, pigeon plum, tourist tree (*gumbo limbo*), cedar, bay berry, horseflesh, wild pine, wild coffee, plumed fern, whisk fern, mistletoe, and ribbon fern.

Example Locations: High coppice, London Creek Ridge; low coppice, the Atallta and Maidenhair coppices. Maideenhair can be very good for birding, but go with a guide to get you to the right spot.

Birds: Black-and-White Warbler, Ovenbird, Hooded Warbler, Red-legged Thrush, Great Lizard Cuckoo; are all likely to be seen along with Black-throated Blue and Black-throated Green Warblers.

PINELAND COMMUNITY

Pineland is the only community that has been commercially developed on the island. The Androsian Bahamian pines were harvested for lumber and pulp wood until 1975. The Bahamian pine is readily identified as it has two to three needles per bundle on its branches, and its pine cones do not fall from the trees, which may be 50 feet high and 2 feet in diameter.

One important feature that made this pine so valuable was that it is termite resistant due to the heavy and dense nature of the wood. Nails and screws go in readily while the tree is still green. After it dries out, however, it is nearly impossible to nail through without drilled pilot holes.

Typical Flora includes: Wild criava, thatch leaf or bow top palm, Bahamian passion flower, white-topped sedge, five fingers, poisonwood, eerodia, yellow allsmanda, bamboo vine, yellow-alder, love vine, rubber vine or devil potato, pine pick, coontie or cycad, manilla sisal or century pant, bracken fern, parsley fern, and anemie fern.

Example Locations: Most of the high interior of Andros.

Birds: Flycatchers, Warblers (Pine, Prairie, Cape May, Yellow-throated, Magnolia), Merlin, Black-faced Grassquit, Hairy Woodpecker and Blue-grey Gnatcatchers are all common.

CULTIVATED GARDEN PLANTS

This community has been added to the list because our participants need to recognize it. It includes several plant species cultivated for human use, including herbal remedies. Many of these were introduced by humans through the Bahamas Agricultural Research Center (BARC), established in the 1970s by Penn State University for pasture crops and livestock feed. BARC closed, due to lack of funding, in 1990, but its legacy is still growing.

In the past, agricultural areas and land that had been cleared for planting by cutting the natural underbrush and burning it were left exposed. These soils generally wear out after a few plantings, and new farms must be cleared. It was BARC's goal to find the means and crops to halt this erosion of the precious little native soil and to encourage subsistence farming among the locals. They have been partially successful.

Cultivated plants include:

- Eddy: Tuber, cooked like potato; the leaves may be more than a foot long.
- Cassava: Some sweet, others bitter. Used like potatoes; poison must be removed from bitter ones.
- Aloe: Used for skin burns; sap from leaves is taken orally for respiratory ailments.
- Sugar cane, papaya, sugar apple.

- Pigeon pea: Rich in protein. When cooked with rice it is the *national dish of the Bahamas*.
- Yam: Grown in groups under leafy vines. Boiled with meat or other vegetables.
- Sour sop: Eaten raw, mixed with milk to form a punch, or used as flavoring for ice cream.
- Sour lime: Used to season fish. *Makes good limeade*.
- Sapodilla (-dilli): Rough brown skin with sweet orange-colored pulp when ripe in spring.
- Guava: Fruit is yellow outside and pink inside; used in making jelly and ice cream.
- Banana: Each plant produces one bunch of bananas and then is cut down. Some varieties are cooked with vegetables and meat; others are baked in bread. These are not the same variety most Americans are used to buying in supermarkets; those are from South America.
- Mango: People with allergies should proceed with caution. The tree belongs to same family as poisonwood.
- Tamarind: Pulp can be mixed with sugar to make a sauce that is eaten like Americans eat applesauce or cranberry sauce. Seeds are sweet.

Birds: Song birds typically love one of three things—(1) fruit, (2) flowers, (3) bugs. Fruits attract bugs. Flowers attract bugs. Where there are bugs there are flycatchers, warblers, and vireos. Where there is fruit there are orioles, Western Spindalis, and tanagers. Where there are flowers you will find hummingbirds and bananaquits. In short, birding in areas with cultivated plants can be exceptionally productive.

SUMMARY TABLE

	Coastal Rock	Sea Strand	Coastal Coppice	Whiteland	Fresh Water	Tidal Flats	Mangrove	Blackland	Pineland	Cultivated	Grass\Savannah
Red Bays			X	X	X	X	X		X	X	
Jungle Pond								X	X		
Joulter's		X				X	X				
Lowes Sound						X	X				
Money Point	X	X					X				
Morgan's Bluff and Cave	X	X	X								
Nicholls Town		X					X	X		XX	
Conch Sound							X				
Mastic Point							X	X		X	
San Andros Airport					X					X	X
Mennonite Farms										X	X
BAMRI				X				X		X	X
London Creek				X			X				
Owen's Town				X				X	X	X	X
Stafford Creek			X	X					X	X	
Blanket Sound (Forfar)					X				X	X	
Gobi Lake					X			X	X		
Staniard Creek			X			X	X			X	
Small Hope Bay							X	X		X	
Calabash Bay and ponds	X				X	X	X				
Fresh Creek		X	X							X	
Blue Holes NP					X			X	X		
Twin Lakes					X				X		
Tarpon Pond		X			X		X				
AUTEC										X	
Cargill Creek			X				X				
Bearing Point		X			X		X				
West Side NP			X		X	X	X				

Note: The plant communities identified in each of the locations are not exhaustive. The communities listed above are those that are either predominant or obvious. For example, the Twin Lakes area has several plant communities in proximity, but the most obvious and important (in terms of birds) are fresh water and pineland communities.

CHAPTER THREE

BIRDING HOT SPOTS

This chapter is intended to provide guidance to the possible locations of specific birds. Before we get into that, let's talk a little bit about how this chapter is organized. First, we note the difficulty of access to the site, as well as the recommended duration of an excursion, which does not include travel time. Also, each location has a table in which specific birds are listed. There are three categories: *Should Find it Here, Might Find it Here, Unlikely to see it anywhere (but this is your best chance)*.

The first category, *Should find it here*, points out birds that are found in relatively *few* places, but commonly found in the specified location. This category will not include ubiquitous birds, like the Black-faced Grassquit, Palm Warbler, Turkey Vulture, Northern Mockingbird, and Common Ground Dove. In fact, these birds will not appear on any specific location list because they are so common that it does not make sense to include them on any one particular location list. Birds with a "rarity rating" of one or two will not make a location target list, either. The birds listed in this category are observed on more than 70 percent of bird-watching trips in this area.

The second category, *Might find it here*, consists of birds that are uncommon at a particular location but are recorded at that location more frequently than at most other sights. The birds listed are observed on less than 50 percent but more than 10 percent of bird-watching trips.

The last category, *Unlikely to see it anywhere (but this is your best chance),* are the unicorns, the "lifers," the birds we have seen very rarely overall but *have* recorded at a particular location.

In addition to the bird table, we have included a location description and GPS coordinates for specific hotspots or areas that we know to be particularly good for birding, based on the vegetative zone or specific features.

As stated previously, the targets listed at any location are not intended to represent a complete list of what can be seen at each location. For example, Owens Town has relatively few "targets," but a good day at Owens Town can easily yield seventy species.

RED BAYS

Ease of Access: Easy (except for the mudflats, which require scuba boots and would be considered difficult)
Duration: 2-3 hours without a trip to the mudflats, 4-5 with mudflats included

Should find it here	Green Heron Black-Bellied Plover Royal Tern Piping Plover* Snowy Plover* Semi-palmated Plover* Western and White Rumped Sandpipers* Sanderlings Western Spindalis Tree Swallow Yellow-throated Warbler Ovenbird Snowy Egret
Might find it here	Pied Billed Grebe Yellow Warbler Northern Parula Hooded Warbler Solitary Sandpiper Red-legged Thrush Great Lizard Cuckoo Least Grebe Bahama Swallow Worm Eating Warbler
Unlikely to see it anywhere (but this is your best chance)	Mangrove Warbler

* During low-tide

On the far west side of the island lies the community of Red Bays. It is as unique in culture and history as it is in birdlife. The road to Red Bays begins approximately 2.5 miles north of San Andros Airport and is marked.

Within 4 miles of the intersection of Queen's Highway and Red Bays Road, a noticeable change in vegetation takes place. Pine Forest gives way to swash. For the purposes of this book, Red Bays begins here.

The habitat to the north and south of the road is excellent for egrets, ducks, grebes, and swallows. This is where you are most likely to find the Bahama Swallow, sometimes sitting on a wire above the road, but more often flying in the skies above. Also, look in the roadside ditches! This is prime "grebe and moorhen" habitat.

The settlement of Red Bays is particularly interesting thanks to the plantings of Ms. Marshall. Ms. Marshall was a bush granny who was very well known for her natural healing concoctions. To make these medicines, she had to have the ingredients, which she planted in her yard and in other areas. As good as those plants are for various treatments, they are at least that good at attracting birds!

A visit to the Marshall Family homestead can yield some fantastic birds. Otis Marshall, who lives across the street from Ms. Marshall's property, is an exceptional source of information. If you tell him "Birdman Joe" sent you, he will tell you some of his best places to see rare species.

At the end of the road (literally at the very furthest point west one can drive) is a dock. Directly to the east of the dock is a very small pond that should produce a Green Heron and Common Yellowthroat.

A short walk north of there is a unique vegetative community that includes sea strand and mangrove to the northeast. These areas can be productive. In fact, in the early 2000s (2002 and 2003), we observed a Mangrove Warbler in this mangrove. So (like all birders), we check out this mangrove every single time we bird watch there, hoping it still visits.

The mudflat south of the dock is productive at low tide. It is a very slippery walk, not for the faint of heart, but worth it if you are into shorebirds.

JUNGLE POND

Ease of Access: Moderately difficult
Duration: 1.5 hours, including hike to site

Jungle Pond is included here to appease any botanist you might have packed in your suitcase and brought along. It is a fascinating area with some amazing plants. Those plants do, in fact, attract birds but none so unique that they warrant special mention here.

Jungle Pond, however, is a one-of-a-kind place. What is very likely an ancient and very small blue hole has filled in, producing a depressed area in the middle of the pine forest. This damp environment is ideal for a variety of epiphytes and orchids. The birds are mostly those that visit from the surrounding pine yard, though the commonly recorded Bahama Yellowthroat is most likely staying in and around Jungle Pond. Blue-grey Gnatcatchers and Thick-billed Vireos also abound. Jungle Pond is not easy to find, and we recommend taking someone with you who knows how to get there.

JOULTER CAYS (THE JOULTERS)

Easy of Access: Difficult
Duration: Plan for a full day

Should find it here	Ring-Billed Gulls Black-Bellied Plover Royal Tern Piping Plover Snowy Plover Semi-palmated Plover Western and White Rumped Sandpiper Sanderlings Semipalmated Sandpiper Dowitchers Wilson's Plover
Might find it here	Baird's Sandpiper Great Black-backed Gull
Unlikely to See it Anywhere (but this is your best chance)	Magnificent Frigate Bird

The Joulters are extraordinary, but they are not particularly easy to get to. You must find someone to take you there by boat, and it can be a pretty long day once you are there. Nevertheless, any naturalist would love to visit this truly unique ecosystem. At low tide the birding can be fantastic, but if you are at the Joulters you might as well enjoy the fish, the sharks, and the astonishing geology that surrounds you.

If you go to the Joulters, bring lots of water, food for the day, and sunscreen. It can be an exhausting day simply because hiking around in shallow water is tiring.

There are not a lot of passerines (perching birds) to be found here, but shorebirds are plentiful. Make sure to check prop roots for birds as well.

Finally, we almost always get something "crazy" flying by (e.g., a Black-Legged Kittiwake in 1996) when we go to the

Joulters. You are almost guaranteed a "beer bird" if you keep your eyes open while you're there.

LOWE SOUND

Ease of Access: Easy
Duration: 2-4 hours (depending on how good the birding is)

Should find it here	House Sparrow (sadly) Herring Gull Ring Billed Gull Royal Tern Willet Little Blue Heron Yellow-crowned Night Heron Greater Yellowlegs Prairie Warbler Cape May Warbler Northern Parula American Kestrel Spotted Sandpiper
Might find it here	Reddish Egret Painted Bunting Lesser Yellowlegs Great Blue Heron Tricolored Heron Osprey
Unlikely to See it Anywhere (but this is your best chance)	Caspian Tern Great Black-backed Gull

Lowe Sound can be spectacular in terms of bird-watching. There are so many little nooks and crannies to explore, and each one of them can yield an exciting find.

There are a few birds that we have recorded here and nowhere else on the island. One such bird is the invasive House Sparrow (which we would rather not see). Other great finds here are the occasional Caspian Tern and the variety of gulls that pass through.

Lowe Sound is a fishing town, and the presence of fish, conch, and their remnants attracts gulls and other birds. It is not surprising to find shorebirds and seafaring birds, but what is remarkable is the presence of so many passerines (perching birds) in the town.

There are a few trees that, when fruiting, attract hundreds of birds of all varieties. In 2014 we recorded twenty-eight species of birds feeding in a fig tree in Lowe Sound. Also, check the prop roots of the mangroves on the south side of town (see below), as there are almost always Greater Yellowlegs and Willets somewhere in them. Below is a list of "must-stop places" in Lowe Sound with GPS coordinates:

- Large Mangrove in Creek next to bridge: 25.148022, -78.065178
- Mudflat on NE corner of Lowe Sound: 25.15473, -78.070631
- Athletic Field: 25.15312, -78.080228 (Pair of American Kestrels)
- Mangroves on South side of town (prop roots are good for Willets): 25.152010, -78.085929
- Fruiting Trees: 25.15441, -78.090643
- Western Tip of Settlement: 25.157462, -78.091894 (Willets and Gulls)

MONEY POINT

Ease of Access: Difficult
Duration: 1-2 Hours

Money Point is an incredible place to explore. We *highly* recommend that you go with someone who knows the area well. Even if you are not staying at Forfar Field Station, see if you can coordinate a trip through them. Money Point is a great place to see a vast variety of marine invertebrates if you know where to look, so it helps to have an expert with you.

Now, the reason we go there is to see birds, and the prize at this location is the American Oystercatcher. This is one of three places on the island where it can be seen fairly regularly. The ponds on the way to Money Point can be quite good for Least Grebe and wading birds.

The GPS coordinates for Money Point are 25.181201, -78.061585. To get there, take the road to Morgan's Bluff (the road leading north from Lowe Sound); then, make a left on a sand road approximately 1.5 miles north of Lowe Sound.

MORGAN'S BLUFF AND CAVE

Ease of Access: Moderate
Duration: 1 hour

Should find it here	Brown Pelican Ring-billed Gull Laughing Gull (Spring and Summer) Spotted Sandpiper Prairie Warbler (Cave) Magnolia Warbler (Cave) Bananaquit (Cave)

Might find it here	Solitary Sandpiper Black-crowned Nightheron (Cave) Yellow-crowned Nightheron (Cave) Greater Antillean Bullfinch (Cave) Yellow-throated Viero (Cave) Yellow-throated Warbler (Cave)
Unlikely to See it Anywhere…(but this is your best chance)	Magnificent Frigatebird

Morgan's Bluff and Cave are both really neat things to see, irrespective if there are birds present. The cave can be explored. The entrance is large and the exit is tiny, so if you are claustrophobic you may not want to crawl the entire length of the cave.

Just past the cave is the bluff. It is the highest point on the island and will require some climbing. The coastal rock vegetative community offers relatively little in the way of food for birds, but the bluff provides a great lookout for pelagic species, which we have recorded here on numerous occasions.

The cave area has a great coppice environment that is fantastic for bird watching. We have found birding here to be highly variable. It is one of those places where it is either hot or cold. There is no in between. If it is cold, go explore the cave and create a great memory that way.

NICHOLL'S TOWN

Ease of Access: Easy to Moderate
Duration: 2-3 hours

Should find it here	Barn Owl Bahama Woodstar Red-legged Thrush Rock Dove Eurasian Collard Dove White Crowned Pigeon American Kestrel Cuban Emerald Magnolia Warbler Black-throated Green Warbler Greater Antillean Bullfinch American Redstart Black-and-White Warbler
Might find it here	Red-Tailed Hawk Scaup (at retention ponds) Ring-necked Duck (retention ponds) Red-winged Blackbird Cape May Warbler
Unlikely to See it Anywhere…(but this is your best chance)	Mangrove Cuckoo Black Whiskered Vireo Least Bittern

Nicholl's Town is actually quite large and quite diverse in terms of plant communities. There are a number of good stops throughout the area. We typically stop first at the retention ponds where Queen's Highway T's into the east-west road leading to Nicholl's Town and Lowe Sound. The ponds sometimes have ducks or grebes in them, so it is always worth a quick check.

The second, and often the most productive in terms of number of species is the neighborhood on the northeast side of town. The GPS coordinates (25.146538, -78.006705) will get you to a little side road in the neighborhood. Park here and walk around in the immediate area. Some of the people in the neighborhood actually feed birds or leave out bird baths. Since there are so many ornamental and flowering plants, the Bananaquits and hummingbirds can be thick through here. We often get White Crowned Pigeons in tree tops in this area. It is excellent for warblers as well.

Another great spot in Nicholl's Town is, quite literally, a hidden gem. It is a freshwater blue hole environment with lots of fantastic coppice surrounding it. Most people call it Ben's Blue Hole, but it has other local names as well. It is on private property and, even though the people who live there are incredibly nice, you should ask before going on the property.

The blue hole has two caves that are close by. The larger of the caves is a roost for a pair of barn owls. We first started spotting the owls here in 1994 and it is likely they were here long before that. Evidence of the owls is all over the rim of the blue hole. Bones from thousands of mice, rats, lizards, and other critters can be found littering the rim.

The coppice is fantastic birding for all sorts of birds, including vireos. The Black Whiskered Vireo was observed here on more than one occasion.

The complex is in the general area of 25.149101, -78.009001, but we recommend you go with a guide to this property.

Overall, Nicholl's Town can be a great stop, especially if you are hungry. Grab a fantastic hamburger at Grizzly's on the way into town or get some amazing Bahamian fare at Sly Fox's on the beach. Also, try to walk around a bit in the town. We always see something interesting in Nicholl's Town. The Pineville Store on the west side of town normally has single serving ice cream on hand. This might be a good place to pay off a 'birding wager'.

CONCH SOUND

Ease of Access: Easy
Duration: 1 hour (2 Hours if you snorkel)

Should find it here	Louisiana Waterthrush Little Blue Heron White Ibis (on the road)
Might find it here	Royal Tern Osprey Northern Waterthrush
Unlikely to See it Anywhere...(but this is your best chance)	Great White (Wunderman's) Heron

Conch Sound is a great place to see the Louisiana Waterthrush. To get there, go south out of Nicholl's Town on the eastern-most road (called Conch Sound Road, but the signage may not be obvious).

The road ends at Conch Sound Blue Hole (25.115354, -78.000367). This marine blue hole is a great snorkel and is a 50 foot swim from the beach. If you go to Conch Sound, pack your mask and snorkel (you don't even need fins) and check out the giant Spadefish and Nurse Shark that hang out around the blue hole.

After a quick snorkel, walking west you will find a great trail and probably a Louisiana Waterthrush. If you are insanely lucky you might see his cousin, the Northern Waterthrush. If you are the luckiest person alive, you will see the Wunderman's Heron. If you see all those and a unicorn, put down your binoculars and walk away…because it will never get better than that.

We do see Osprey and the occasional Peregrine Falcon around Conch Sound. We also find the White-eyed Vireo in the thicket behind the church located at 25.117308, -77.996950.

MASTIC POINT

Ease of Access: Easy
Duration: 2-4 hours

Should find it here	Smooth-billed Ani
	Brown Pelican
	Little Blue Heron
	Snowy Egret
	White Ibis
	Western Spindalis
	Mourning Dove
	Zenaida Dove
	American Kestrel
	Spotted Sandpiper
Might find it here	Ring-necked Duck
	Blue-winged Teal

	American Oystercatcher
	Osprey (nesting)
	Bahama Swallow
	Scaup
	Sora
	Royal Tern
	Herring Gull
	Hairy Woodpecker
	Merlin
	Yellow Warbler
Unlikely to See it Anywhere...(but this is your best chance)	Ruddy Duck Cuban Crow Redhead Duck

This is Nick's favorite place on the entire island. No matter when we go to Mastic Point we always see something crazy. A pair of Cuban crows in 2014 was perhaps one of our most exciting discoveries. But others include Bufflehead, Swainson's Warbler, Green-winged Teal, Virginia and Black Rail and many more.

Mastic does not give up her gifts too easily. One has to work for the birds. The roadside ponds on the way into Mastic Point from San Andros airport can be great for ducks and rails. We have gotten such rarities as Green-Winged Teal, American Wigeon, and other ducks out of those ponds, but Blue-Winged Teal and American Coots can be relied upon.

Once you get into Mastic Point there are a few places to go. The south end of Mastic Point has incredible mangrove, seastrand, and coastal coppice habitat. Wading birds, shorebirds, gulls, and terns are all possibilities. Also, nesting Bahama Swallows can be found in the area around the pink church. Cuban Crows and Red-Tailed Hawks have been spotted here as well.

In Mastic Point proper, there is a gas station (they have cold drinks and Little Debbie Snack Cakes...we love Little Debbies) owned by Patrick Romer. Mr. Romer keeps pretty good track of the birds coming in and out of Mastic Point Pond.

The small park across the street from the gas station is a great place to set up a spotting scope and look at the water and mangroves. Snowy Egrets like to hang out on the far side of the pond, as do American Coots and some ducks.

There is a large mangrove "island" directly in front of the gas station. At dusk, hundreds, if not thousands, of doves race into the mangrove to roost along with many White Ibis. It is a sight to behold. The exact coordinates of the mangrove are: 25.052712, -77.980130.

No trip to Mastic Point is complete without visiting the harbor. The drive to the harbor from the gas station is about 2 miles (harbor GPS: 25.071526, -77.965902). The harbor is your best chance to see a Spotted Sandpiper and a Brown Pelican and a manatee! You read correctly! In January 2014 we spotted a manatee in the tiny Mastic Point harbor. The bushes in front of the harbor are also very good for Western Spindalis and other song birds.

The road along the beach (between the dock and the harbor) always seems to produce something good. There will be Anis and likely an American Kestrel or two trying to eat the Anis, but even beyond that you should find some nice birds.

Oystercatchers are not here on a majority of trips, but common enough that you should look for them, especially by the docks and harbor. A Little Blue Heron hangs out on the sunken ship in the harbor, so look for him as well.

Lastly, in town, just a little south of the school, look for figs or Sapodilla trees with fruit. Birds flock to these trees under such conditions, therefore you should as well.

SAN ANDROS AIRPORT

Ease of Access: Highly Accessible, but you must have prior permission to birdwatch at the pond
Duration: 1-2 Hours

Should find it here	Killdeer Cattle Egret Limpkin Common Moorhen Yellow-rumped Warbler Merlin Yellow-bellied Sapsucker
Might find it here	Sora Hood Merganser Bahama Oriole Burrowing Owl (at night) Baltimore Oriole Indigo Bunting Red Tailed Hawk
Unlikely to See it Anywhere…(but this is your best chance)	West Indian Whistling Duck Grasshopper Sparrow Eastern Meadowlark

This is a "must do" birdwatching stop. Arriving early in the morning and being patient is important. There will be an eruption at some point, you just have to be patient.

There will be lots of Yellow-Rumped Warblers, Northern Mockingbirds, Palm Warblers, and Black-faced Grassquits. There will also be a lot of other really great birds as well.

Bird the whole area and the fields close to the airport as well. There are usually some nice Emberizids (sparrows) in and around the airport property. Sparrows are not very sexy to people who come for the United States (where sparrows are very common), but on North Andros sparrows are hard to come by, and your best chance is the areas around the airport.

MENNONITE FARM

GPS Coordinate: 25.023020, 78.037746
Ease of Access: Easy, just ask before you bird watch
Duration: 1 hour

Should find it here	White-winged Dove Eurasian Collard Dove Mourning Dove Zenaida Dove Cattle Egret
Might find it here	Red-tailed Hawk Indigo Bunting Hooded Warbler
Unlikely to See it Anywhere…(but this is your best chance)	Sandhill Crane (actually down the road a bit)

Ask David (property manager) if it is OK to birdwatch, and while you are at it, tell him "Birder Joe" says "Hello!" The Mennonite Farm has a great orchard that can be productive, but the short drive along the fields toward the back of the property can be worth it as well.

Hang out long enough near the orchard and you are bound to see a White-winged dove. You might even see a Merlin chasing it!

Just to the north of the orchard, there is a thicket in the mixed vegetation next to the pine stand. Finding your way into the low understory can be very productive for warblers. We have gotten Hooded Warblers in this spot about 30% of our visits.

In the early 2000s a pair of Sandhill cranes was reported just to the east of the Mennonite Farms, but have not been seen since to our knowledge (though we check the property every winter, just in case).

BAHAMAS AGRICULTURAL AND MARINE INSTITUTE

GPS Coordinate: 24.961573,-78.023560
Ease of Access: Easy
Duration: 3 hours, but you will go more than one day

Should find it here	Painted Bunting
	Hooded Warbler
	Bahama Oriole
	Indigo Bunting
	Limpkin
	Cape May Warbler

	Yellow-throated Warbler Prarie Warbler Red Legged Thrush Grey Catbird
Might find it here	Pine Wabler Yellow-throated Vireo White-eyed Vireo Grasshopper Sparrow Tawny-shouldered 　Blackbird Summer Tanager Merlin
Unlikely to See it Anywhere…(but this is your best chance)	A Unicorn

This place is incredible. Early in the morning it is one of the best places in the entire Bahamas to bird watch. You can leave this venue with 35-40 species in a 2-3 hour walk. One fruiting fig or sapodilla will host 15-30 species alone.

Recently, the College of the Bahamas has invested substantially in the property, turning it into a true University environment. We feared that this construction might take away from the bird life on the property. We are happy to report that, at least to date, this has not been the case.

There are many species of warblers, vireos, and other songbirds that can be found here, but none is as sought after as the Painted Bunting. Now, before we tell you the secret honey hole for the Painted Bunting (or P-Bizzle, as we like to call him), you have to promise to never give the secret away to anyone who has not bought this book. That seems fair, right? Ok, P-Bizzle and his fantastically handsome buddy (the Hooded Warbler) can be found around the following GPS coordinate: 24.956689, -78.027364, or the southeast corner of the property. Be patient. Both species will respond to their calls.

Some people say it is unethical to imitate a bird's call to see it better. The truth of the matter is that these birds are foraging and flitting around anyway. They are not trying to establish a breeding territory. If you imitate their call and they pop up from a bug or berry meal it really is inconsequential to the survival of that bird.

Now, when the birds are in breeding season or calling because they are on territory it would NOT BE OK to imitate their call. So, as Nick always says, "Please pish responsibly."

OWENS TOWN

GPS Coordinate: 24.87515, --78.035277
Ease of Access: Moderate-Difficult
Duration: 4 hours

Should find it here	La Sagra's Flycatcher
	Stolid Flycatcher
	Loggerhead Kingbird
	Magnolia Warbler
	Pine Warbler
	Black-throated Green Warbler
	Blue-grey gnatcatcher
	Red-Legged Thrush
	Great Lizard Cuckoo

	Thick-billed Vireo White-eyed Vireo Common Yellowthroat Bahama Yellowthroat Bahama Oriole Cattle Egret
Might find it here	Peregrine Falcon Bobwhite Quail Red-tailed Hawk Key West Quail Dove Bahama Woodstar Worm-eating Warbler Blue-headed Vireo Great Crested Flycatcher
Unlikely to See it Anywhere…(but this is your best chance)	Black-Whiskered Vireo Eastern Phoebe Blue-winged Warbler Vesper Sparrow Yellow-breasted Chat Eastern Meadowlark Cedar Waxwing

By far the most biologically diverse community on North Andros Island, this hotspot can easily produce 50 species in a 4 hours trip. Our record (though it was for a 24 hour period) was 82 species. The list of "possibilities" is honestly too big to print. It is really important to be patient in this place. Feeding flocks move through and it is common to go from not seeing anything to having 15 species around you in no time. The best days at Owens Town are the mild days with just a slight overcast. Add in a rain the night before and you are in business!

The secret to Owens Town is the mixed communities. Pine forest next to savannah, next to brackish tidal creek with mangroves, next to cultivated plants produces a very rich environment for birds.

The specialty at this location has to be the Swainson's Warbler. Walk into the former settlement from the "main entrance." The houses have long since burned down, but the foundations and many of the ornamental plants and fruit trees remain. The foundations hold water and the dense foliage provides a great humid thicket environment where the Swainson's Warbler thrives. In 2015 we recorded 5 individuals in the area near the first set of foundations to the north of the "main entrance." Possibilities abound at Owens Town. You may have to work for them, but Owens Town rarely disappoints.

LONDON CREEK

Ease of Access: Easy
Duration: 10-15 minutes

London Creek is a relatively quick stop along the way to or from Owens Town. Common Yellowthroat are usually found in the area, but the real prize is the open water to the west of the road. There's a mangrove that sometimes hold Blue-wing Teal and American Coots.

Occasionally Ring-necked ducks have been seen further downstream. Egrets and herons are also commonly found here.

Roseate Spoonbill's have been reported on the east side of the road in the ponds just north of London Creek. Be forewarned: There is a stick along the north side of the creek a couple hundred meters west of the road that looks remarkably like a heron. Joe has had to convince Nick on at least 10 different occasions that this "Great Blue Heron" was actually a stick.

London Creek is what we call a quick hit. It is not worthy of a lot of time, but can produce a good bird or two.

STAFFORD CREEK

Ease of Access: Easy
Duration: 1-2 hours at night

Should find it here	Burrowing Owl Cuban Emerald Western Spindalis Royal Tern Black-crowned Night Heron Yellow-crowned Night Heron
Might find it here	Bahama Yellowthroat Barn Owl Brown Pelican

Unlikely to See it Anywhere…(but this is your best chance)	Swainson's Warbler

Stafford Creek offers two species that are easily found there and difficult to find anywhere else. The Burrowing Owl and the Antillean Nighthawk can both be found at the school yard in Stafford creek on almost any given night. The Burrowing Owl is extremely curious and will respond to a reasonable imitation of its call. The Nighthawk can often be found perched on a stick or pipe anywhere near the light in the schoolyard.

Stafford Creek also has a Black-crowned Night Heron that prefers to hunt near the bridge across from "Love at First Sight Hotel." During the day the creek in front of the hotel can produce many types of water birds. Gulls, pelicans, terns, wading birds, Osprey, and others can be seen here.

There is also a very tiny freshwater blue hole immediately to the north of Love at First Sight. We have seen Swainson's Warblers there, but more commonly find Bahama Yellowthroat and an occasional Waterthrush.

The logging road that is just to the south of the creek can be productive in the morning. Western Spindalis, Blue-grey Gnatcatcher, and Cuban Emerald and Cresent-eyed peewee are very common.

About a mile north of Stafford Creek is the Stafford creek dump. Birdwatching at a dump does not sound too glamorous, but it is actually a pretty great spot to see some good birds. We have had pretty good success calling in Barn owls around the dump. It is truly thrilling to see a giant owl swoop over your head in the middle of the night (even if you are at a dump). It is also a great place to see a Yellow-crowned Night Heron at night. The dump is also a pretty good place to birdwatch during the day. There are a lot of insects around, which usually means a lot of warblers and vireos.

FORFAR FIELD STATION

Ease of Access: Easy
Duration: 1-3 hours

Should find it here	Osprey Pelican Reddish Egret Ovenbird Yellow-bellied Sapsucker Yellow-Throated Warbler Black-Throated Blue Warbler Black-and-White Warbler
Might find it here	Worm-Eating Warbler Hooded Warbler Hairy Woodpecker White Crowned Pigeon
Unlikely to See it Anywhere...(but this is your best chance)	

One nice thing about staying at Forfar Field Station as many times as we have is that we have more notes about this property than perhaps any other location on the island. The great thing about Forfar is that whether you bird watch for 15 minutes or a couple of hours you can always get nice birds. The beach will provide excellent views of Royal Terns, Reddish Egrets (especially at low tide on the sandbar to the north side of Blanket Sound), and the occasional shorebirds that fly up from Staniard Creek. Osprey and Brown Pelicans are also more likely here than other places on the island.

Behind the field station, on the south side of the circular drive, is a thicket. This is directly adjacent to the compost and trash collection area. Honestly, it is not the most pleasant smelling area to birdwatch, but it will, most certainly, produce an incredible amount of warblers. Worm Eating Warblers, Hooded Warblers, Ovenbirds, American Redstart, and Black-throated Blue Warbler's are not uncommon here. Both Hairy Woodpeckers and Yellow-bellied Sapsuckers are common, especially on the West Indian almond trees.

The cultivated areas on the front (west side) of the property offer excellent views of Northern Parula and Crescent-eyed (Cuban) Peewee. Also, there is a trail that wanders through a coastal coppice area. We typically find Red-legged Thrush, Great Lizard Cuckoos, White Crowned Pigeon, and a number of other species. If you are staying at Forfar make sure you check out the area directly behind the "motel" units. It can be quite good early in the morning.

SOUTH BLANKET SOUND

Ease of Access: Easy-Moderate
Duration: 1 hour

South Blanket Sound is the first community south of Forfar. To get there, turn left at the first road south of Forfar.

The prize here is the possibility of Clapper Rails. We typically find them by the pond behind school house. This is the best chance of seeing Clapper Rails on the mainland (Pigeon Cay also has a pair, but getting to those birds requires a boat trip).

At the far east end of town, where the road turns into sand, is a seastrand/mangrove complex that can be quite good for shorebirds and waiting birds. We have recorded the Clapper Rails there as well.

The settlement itself is worth walking around. It is really only one road, so if you find a nice thicket or flowering tree, you should stop and take a look. We have found many great lizard cuckoos sitting along the road in thick, coppice like areas.

GOBI LAKE

Ease of Access: Moderate- Difficult
Duration: 2-3 hours

Should find it here	Blue-winged Teal Common Moorhen American Coot Sora Bahama Yellowthroat Common Yellowthroat
Might find it here	Scaup Norther Pintail American Wigeon
Unlikely to See it Anywhere…(but this is your best chance)	Purple Gallinule House Wren Cinnamon Teal Key West Quail Dove

Gobi Lake is an amazing spectacle. It is a filled-in freshwater blue hole that has five distinct vegetative communities around it. For many years the area around the lake served as a rookery for hundreds of Little Blue Herons. For whatever reason, the herons have stopped roosting there, but there are still many great birds to be found.

The small pond that is visible at first glance is really only a small part of the "lake." On the north side of the pond is a huge swampy area that can hold number of duck species. One of the most amazing finds in the swampy area was a group of cinnamon teal back in 1996 (here we have to offer a shout out to Andy Pyle for spotting those birds behind a cluster of reeds). We had written off the find as an anomaly, but the birds were spotted again in 2002 in the exact same location. The only time we have observed a Purple Gallinule on North Andros was at Gobi Lake. Same with the House Wren. And, if you are going to see Key West Quail Doves, the far west side of the small pond is as good a place as any.

To get there, one must take the main logging road south from Stafford Creek for about five miles. At (or near) coordinates 24.830700, -77.917970 there is a road heading west. It actually may not look like much of a road, and if you cannot pass it just walk the remnants of the road for about a quarter mile. Gobi Lake can be found at coordinates 24.828527, -77.923028.

WARNING: If you are a high adventure birdwatcher, you might be inclined to walk into the swamp on the north side of the lake. We respect that. In fact, we encourage it. That said, there are lots of little tiny biting shrimp that live in the swamp. They really love the soft flesh between your toes. What we do to ward off these little critters is wear socks underneath our scuba boots. Then, using duct tape, we tape the scuba boots to the socks to seal the scuba boots from invading biting shrimp.

Gobi Lake is a bit of a challenge to get to, and is a difficult site to traverse, but the rewards can be great. For the serious birder who is looking for an oddball species this is a place to go.

STANIARD CREEK

Ease of Access: Difficult
Duration: 2-4 hours

Should find it here	Black-Bellied Plover Piping Plover Snowy Plover Wilson's Plover Semi-palmated Plover Western and White Rumped Sandpipers Least Sandpiper Baird's Sandpiper Pectoral Sandpiper Dowitcher Sanderlings Reddish Egret Snowy Egret Tricolored Heron
Might find it here	Great Egret Tricolored Heron Great Blue Heron
Unlikely to See it Anywhere…(but this is your best chance)	Dunlin Marbled Godwit Hudsonian Godwit

Staniard Creek is one of the most important bird areas in the Caribbean. The huge mud flat, extending from South Blanket Sound all the way to Staniard Creek (which is a distance of several miles), is the feature that makes it so special. On the way to Staniard Creek, driving south from Forfar, and extensive mangrove area opens on the east side of the road. This area can be productive for Great Egrets, Great Blue Herons, Snowy Egrets, Reddish Egrets, and the occasional Tricolored Heron.

The first left past the mangroves (which is approximately 6 miles south of Forfar) is the road to Staniard Creek. After less than a mile, the road will "T". Turning right at the "T" will take you to the east side of the creek and the main part of the settlement. Turning left will take you along the creek towards a dead-end.

This is normally our launching point to get to the mud flats (GPS coordinates: 24.840435, -77.892552). Getting to the mudflat can be very difficult, or very easy, depending on how you choose to access it. If you are staying at Kamalame Cay access is easy, as the mud flat is directly accessible at the end of that property. It seems to us that having throngs of muddy, stinky, and otherwise unsightly of birdwatchers traipsing through a high-end resort is not highly desirable. Because of that, we never ask to use the Kamalame property as a launching point for our mud flat expeditions. To be clear, they are great people (and would probably let us), but that seems a bit much to ask. We find that the best way, and usually the fastest way, to access the mud flat is to grab a dry bag (or two), load our spotting scopes and binoculars, and swim across the creek at the location provided here: 24.842124, -77.893941.

Once on the mud flat it may be several hundred yards until birds are spotted, but the location of the birds is highly dependent on the tide. We have found that the best time to go is proximately 1 1/2 to 2 1/2 hours past low tide. Mixed flocks of shorebirds abound on this extensive mud flat. An hour or two on the mud flat could easily-year-old 30 species of shorebirds and wading birds. Of particular interest are the tricolored Heron, Reddish Egret, Piping Plover, Snowy Plover, and the myriad of sandpipers and other shorebirds that can be spotted here.

It is important to remember that this habitat may be one of the most important areas for wintering shorebirds in the world. Because of this, we are extremely careful not to disrupt the birds or their environment in anyway. A high magnification spotting scope is recommended so that you are not tempted to get too close to the birds while they are foraging. Finally, we have three words of advice for anyone going onto the mud flat: sunscreen, hat, water.

RAINBOW BLUE HOLE

Ease of Access: Moderately difficult
Duration: 1 hour

A couple miles south of Staniard Creek on Queen's Highway is Rainbow Blue Hole. It is east of the road and requires a ½ mile hike on rugged terrain to get there.

If you need to see a Least Grebe, stop by Rainbow. The White-cheeked Pintail also hangs out here as well and the coppice environment leading to the blue hole is great for songbirds. You might also take a swim, but be forewarned that there are the crazy little fish (tiny little dudes, about an inch long) that like to nibble at your dead skin. Nick actually likes it and says they are 'exfoliants' to help him maintain his youthful appearance.

SMALL HOPE BAY

Ease of Access: Easy
Duration: 30 minutes to 1 hour

If you are staying at Small Hope, then take advantage of their nature trail as well as the mangroves immediately to the west of the property. The mangroves are excellent places to find nearly every type of wading bird. If you have not spotted a Little Blue Heron or a Green Heron on your Andros bird expedition and you desperately need one before you leave, this is the place to go. It is also a fairly reliable spot for the Red-winged Blackbird and Tawny-shouldered Blackbird.

BLUE HOLES NATIONAL PARK

Ease of Access: Easy-Difficult depending on where
Duration: 1-4 hours, depending

This is a vast area that can provide a great number of species. It is not a specific location, rather a large swath of land that has a number of different habitats. For the purposes of most birdwatchers, who have only limited time, there are two stops that must be made.

The first is actually not in the National Park, but on the way to it. It is the large lake directly to the west of love hill, on the way into the National Park. This lake (GPS coordinates: 24.704354, -77.844416) has proven to be an excellent spot for ducks. Redhead, Ruddy Ducks, Scaup, Pintail, and Teal have been spotted here with some regularity. The problem is that these ducks are hunted on this lake and judging by the number of shells on the shore it would appear they have been hunted a lot. Ducks, as much as any other animal, are very skittish once they have been hunted and it can take some time for them to return if they have been hunted at a location recently (especially if they were hunted in the evening as opposed to hunted in the morning). Still, it is a spot that has generally been productive for us and is worth a few minutes of your birdwatching time to check it out.

The longer drive is to Church's Blue Hole. Church's Blue Hole is a famous recreational adventure on Andros Island. If you go, make sure you take a bathing suit and be prepared for a wonderful time, with or without birds. The area around the blue hole can be productive for a number of pineland species. Pine Warblers, Blue-gray Gnatcatchers, Prairie Warblers, and Magnolia Warblers should be spotted. The prize, however, is the White-cheeked Pintail that is commonly found here. This species is also found in Rainbow blue hole (directly south of Staniard Creek), but is more reliable here. That said, we have only recorded it here on about 20% of our trips, so it is not a sure thing. What is a sure thing, however, is a good time. The birds here are pretty good, but the water and the environment are what takes the cake!

CALABASH BAY AND PONDS

Ease of Access: Easy
Duration: 1 hour (visit often!)

Should find it here	Blue-winged Teal Common Moorhen American Coot Sora Least Grebe Ring-necked Duck Black-bellied Plover Ruddy Turnstone
Might find it here	Black-necked Stilt Pied-billed Grebe American Bittern Yellow-crowned Night Heron American Oystercatcher
Unlikely to See it Anywhere...(but this is your best chance)	American Wigeon

South of Small Hope Bay are Calabash Bay and Ponds. The ponds are on the east side of the road and are north of the bay. The ponds are small enough that if you are not paying attention you could miss them. These ponds are absolutely essential to any birdwatching adventure on Andros Island.

The northernmost pond (which is just a couple hundred meters north of the densely foliated south pond) is a reliable spot for Least Grebe, Common Moorhen, Blue-Winged Teal, Ring-Necked Duck, and a number of songbirds. If you are to see a Black-Necked Stilt on Andros, you are most likely to find it in either of the two ponds or on Calabash Bay itself.

The north pond is a somewhat reliable spot for American Bittern.

This birding hotspot is very accessible and can produce different birds at different times of day. Since it is right off of the main road it makes sense to stop at it every time you drive by. It is important to pull off of the road if you stop. The ponds are on a dangerous curve. Give cars enough room to pass.

Calabash Bay can be an excellent spot for shorebirds, Night Herons, Ruddy Turnstones, American Oystercatchers, and Black-necked Stilts. None of these birds will be there much before or after low tide. The secret to fantastic finds at Calabash Bay is getting there as soon as the rocks are exposed. The feeding window at this location is smaller than at other tidal flats.

FRESH CREEK, ANDROS TOWN, ANDROSIA

Ease of Access: Easy-Difficult (seeing into Tarpon Pond)
Duration: 2-3 hours

Should find it here	Common Moorhen American Coot Sora Least Grebe Ring-necked Duck Black-bellied Plover Ruddy Turnstone White Ibis Tree Swallow Black-throated Blue Warbler

	Magnolia Warbler Prairie Warbler
Might find it here	Cattle Egret Bahama Swallow Painted Bunting Yellow-throated Vireo White-eyed Vireo
Unlikely to See it Anywhere…(but this is your best chance)	American Wigeon Blue-headed Vireo Barn Swallow

Fresh Creek (and the settlement of Andros town) provide a number of great birding opportunities. The creek itself is a great place to find Tree Swallows, and the occasional Bahama Swallow (and even once in a while a Barn Swallow). It is very likely that along either side of the creek there will be at least one of the following: Great Blue Heron, Great Egret, Little Blue Heron, Reddish Egret, or Tricolored Heron. Laughing Gulls, Ring-billed Gulls, and the occasional Herring Gull are recorded here as well. Royal Terns are also common.

The settlement itself is a great place to look for birds, and White Ibis and Cattle Egrets can be found in the lawns. There are many fruiting trees, and where there are fruits there are birds. On the south side of the creek there are three major birding hotspots. First, the Lighthouse Club (which is the marina on the south side of the creek) has a couple of giant fig trees in the front lawn of their property. If the figs are fruiting those trees will be loaded with birds.

On the opposite side of the road from the Lighthouse Club is Androsia. Androsia is a batik clothing/fabric company with manufacturing and a retail store on site. The property itself and areas adjacent (directly south) have a number of trees and thickets that make it an excellent stop for warblers and vireos. The morning activity at Androsia can be quite good. The Blue-headed Vireo and Painted Bunting have been spotted here on more than one occasion, but are still quite rare. The Yellow-throated and White-eyed Vireo are more common and would be considered target birds here.

Back to the East, along the beach, there are a number of exposed shoals at low tide. Rudd Turnstones, Black-bellied Plovers, Solitary Sandpipers, and Spotted Sandpipers are commonly seen here.

About a quarter mile south of the lighthouse, about 100 m in from the beach, is a long narrow pond. Locals call it Tarpon Pond, though it may not show up on any map under that name. It has a rather in penetrable mangrove wall around it, which might require an adventurous birder to climb a tree or risk hopping on a mangrove prop root. The water is extraordinarily salinic and we do not recommend wading into the pond. There are a couple of cutouts which might afford some view of the water, but it is so dense with mangroves that it is difficult to see very far. If, however, you can get elevated, and see the water below, you might find Ring-necked ducks, Scaup, Wigeon, Moorhens, Least Grebes, Pied-billed Grebes, and a few passerine birds. Tarpon Pond is not an easy place to bird watch, but there are good birds to be found here with a little work and patience.

AUTEC

Ease of Access: Easy
Duration: 15 minutes

AUTEC is on this list for one reason and one reason only: the West Indian Whistling Duck. There are other birds that can be seen here, but they can all be found elsewhere. The problem with AUTEC is that it is a United States military installation that requires security clearance for entrance. That said, sometimes we see the West Indian Whistling Ducks in proximity of AUTEC, without being on the AUTEC property proper. If you absolutely need a West Indian Whistling Duck try to get a connection at the base. It is your best shot at seeing the species. Keep in mind, however, that AUTEC is a military installation and there are armed guards, so don't jump the fence to get a good look at the West Indian Whistling Duck. They take that sort of stuff pretty seriously.

BOWEN SOUND AND CARGILL CREEK

Ease of Access: Easy*
Duration: 1-2 hours

Should find it here*	Green Heron White Crowned Pigeon Rock Dove Western Kingbird
Might find it here*	Bahama Yellowthroat Bahama Mockingbird Peregrine Falcon Merlin

Unlikely to See it Anywhere…(but this is your best chance)*	Bahama Mockingbird

*Excluding Bowen Sound Flats

The road South from Fresh Creek takes you through an expansive swash and mangrove environment where birds can be seen on either side of the road.

Just to the east of Bowen Sound is a tidal flat that has been productive for shorebirds for us over the years (coordinates 24.612751, -77.751925). It is not particularly easy to get to, as you have to get there by boat, but may be worth a stop at low tide, especially if you are taking a boat out from Bowen Sound.

Cargill Creek, for whatever reason, has been a hotspot for White Crowned Pigeon and Western Kingbird (in the spring). The settlement itself may be good to walk around as it has a number of different plant communities that will support different species of birds. Also, it should be noted that Bahama Mockingbird, which is very rare on North Andros Island, is most commonly seen south of Bowen Sound. We record the Bahama Mockingbird more frequently in Cargill Creek than any other area, though it is not particularly common there either.

The final word about Bowen Sound and Cargill Creek: the people here are extraordinarily kind and knowledgeable. They may not know the technical names of birds, but if you show them a picture of the bird you would like to see they will tell you if it is around and where to find it. These areas do not get visited as much as the northern settlements, but can be just as good for birdwatching

BEHRING POINT

Ease of Access: Easy
Duration: 1-1.5 hours

Behring Point is the southernmost point of North Andros Island. To the east lies the Atlantic Ocean and the barrier reef, to the south lies middle bight and the tidal creek that separates North Andros Island from South Andros Island. Over the years, we have seen some amazing birds in this area. Roseate Spoonbills, every type of wading bird, shorebirds, and the occasional report of a Greater Flamingo make this location worth checking out.

There are also a good number of ornamental in flowering plants in the yards of this settlement. Walking around and exploring can be a great way to find an oddball species. For example, we have recorded the Painted Bunting here on a number of occasions, and done well with other uncommon passerine species as well.

WEST SIDE NATIONAL PARK

Ease of Access: Difficult
Duration: Full day

If your time affords it, we recommend that you coordinate with the local office of the Bahamas National Trust to see if there is a trip going to the West Side National Park. The two hour boat ride from Behring Point to the park may produce some interesting birds, but the reality is that the birdwatching on this trip can be average to poor. That is not, however, why one would make this trip. It is truly one of the most beautiful places you will ever go. The untouched environment is something to behold. The endemic Andros iguana can also be found here and it is truly a remarkable species to behold. We have seen flamingos, spoonbills, and a variety of other birds while traveling through middle bight to West Side National Park, but we do not count on seeing a great number of birds. What is certain on such a trip, however, is a sense of wonder and awe the likes of which one rarely finds in our world today.

CHAPTER FOUR

BIRDS

This chapter gives you specific locations where species have been frequently spotted. *This is not to suggest that all of the species that have been spotted on North Andros are included here.* In fact, we have included only the birds that have a greater than 20% chance of being spotted (based on our records) over a one week birding adventure on North Andros (assuming 8 hours per day of birding). We should tell you there are a few species (e.g. Roseate Spoonbill, Greater Flamingo, Painted Bunting, Grasshopper Sparrow, Tropic Bird, Manx Shearwater and a few others with a rarity of 'five') that are included because we have recorded them a number of times and they are just awesome finds on North Andros. Also, it warrants mentioning again that the data that has informed our "rarity" and "best places to find this bird" categories, comes from the winter and early spring months. Spring and fall migration can be very erratic and the birds are not as reliably found in specific areas during these times.

SHEARWATERS AND PETRELS

Manx Shearwater
Puffinus puffinus
12-15 in. Plate: 1

Wow-Factor   Rarity   Behavior

Best places to find this species: Tongue of the Ocean, anywhere beyond the reef.

Key Features: Black and gray upperparts, white underparts. Glides with wings straight out at sides.

Notes:

Audubon's Shearwater
Puffinus lherminieri
12-13 in. Plate: 1

Wow-Factor   Rarity   Behavior

Best places to find this species: Tongue of the Ocean, anywhere beyond the reef.

Key Features: Dusty-brown upperparts and white underparts. Dark eyes, gray beak, and pink-gray feet with dark nails.

Notes:

Wilson's Storm Petrel
Oceanites oceanicus
6.5-7.5 in. Plate: 1

Wow-Factor	Rarity	Behavior
🪶 🪶	🪶 🪶	🪶 🪶 🪶 🪶

Best places to find this species: Tongue of the Ocean, anywhere beyond the reef.

Key Features: Brown-black body with tuft of white on rear, yellow membrane between toes.

Upper wings are brown-black with a pale bar. Black-tipped underwings with pale patch on coverts. Appears to hop when flying over water (cool behavior!).

Notes:

PELICANS AND TROPIC BIRDS

White-Tailed Tropicbird
Phaethon lepturus
27.5-32.5 in. Plate: 2

Wow-Factor	Rarity	Behavior
🪶 🪶 🪶 🪶 🪶	🪶 🪶 🪶 🪶 🪶	🪶 🪶 🪶

Best places to find this species: Tongue of the Ocean.

Key Features: Long central tail streamer. Mostly white with black wing bars and patches of black on wing tips. Bright-yellow bill and black eye stripe.

Juvenile: Gray in color, yellow-green bill, lacks the long central feathers, black bars on back.

Notes:

Brown Pelican
Pelecanus occidentalis
51 in. Plate: 2

Wow-Factor	Rarity	Behavior
🪶 🪶 🪶 🪶	🪶 🪶 🪶	🪶 🪶 🪶 🪶

Best places to find this species: Mastic Point, the mouth of Stafford Creek, and Morgan's Bluff.

Key Features: Large overall size, distinctive large bill. Dives with great force when hunting fish, stunning the fish (cool behavior!).

Juvenile: Mostly brown throughout with whitish underparts.

Adult: Silver-gray back with dark underparts.

Notes:

FRIGATEBIRD

Magnificent Frigatebird
Fregata magnificens
35-45 in. Plate: 3

Wow-Factor	Rarity	Behavior
🪶 🪶 🪶 🪶 🪶 *	🪶 🪶 🪶 🪶 🪶	🪶 🪶 🪶

Best places to find this species: Staniard Rock and the open ocean.

Key Features: Large in size, pointed black wings, and long slender beak. * = Male in breeding plumage has a bright red chest (gular sac).

Juvenile: White head. Blue-gray legs, feet, and bill. Diamond-shaped patch on underparts.

Males: Red gular sac and purple iridescence to the feathers near the crown.

Breeding Males: Inflated red gular sac.

Females: Blue eye-ring. White breast and sides of neck. Brown wing band.

Notes:

GULLS

Great Black-Backed Gull
Larus marinus
28-31 in. Plate: 4

Wow-Factor	Rarity	Behavior
🖋 🖋 🖋	🖋 🖋 🖋 🖋 🖋	🖋 🖋 🖋

Best places to find this species: Lowe Sound (north side).

Key Features: Giant gull, broad brown-black wings with white tips, white body with large yellow beak. Can be a bit of a bully.

Juvenile: Spotty gray, brown, and white plumage and black bill with whit tip.

Notes:

Ring-billed Gull
Larus delawarensis
17 in. Plate: 4

Wow-Factor	Rarity	Behavior
🖋 🖋	🖋	🖋

Best places to find this species: Lowe Sound and Fresh Creek.

Key Features: Thick black band on bill, black tips on wings, pale iris.

Juvenile: Brown-and-white-speckling coloration throughout. Dark tail. Black tip on bill.

Breeding Adult: White head, breast, and underparts. Gray on back. Pale iris. Wings extend beyond tail and are black at the tip with white spots towards the end. Thick, black band on bill.

Non-breeding Adult: Yellow legs. White on face, neck, and underparts. Gray on back. Slight brown speckling on back of neck. Broad black band on bill.

Notes:

Herring Gull
Larus argentatus
25 in. Plate: 4

Wow-Factor	Rarity	Behavior
🖋 🖋	🖋 🖋 🖋	🖋

Best places to find this species: Lowe Sound.

Key Features: Pink legs and yellow bill with red spot underneath towards tip.

Juvenile: All brown coloration, slightly lighter speckling. Dark bill.

Non-breeding Adult: Extensive streaking on back of neck. White underparts; darker on top.

Breeding Adult: White head and underparts. Gray on back with black primaries.

Notes:

Laughing Gull
Larus articilla
16.5 in. Plate: 4

Wow-Factor	Rarity	Behavior
🪶 🪶 🪶	🪶 🪶	🪶

Best places to find this species: Fresh Creek and any beach in spring or summer.

Key Features: Slight white eye-arcs, black head, deep red bill drooped at the tip. Gray back, black on primaries, and white underparts.

Juvenile: Overall dusky brown color. Dark bill.

Non-breeding Adult: Slight gray streaking on back of head. Black legs and feet.

Breeding Adult: Black primaries with small white tips. Red legs.

Notes:

TERNS

Royal Tern
Thalasseus maximus
20 in. Plate: 7

Wow-Factor	Rarity	Behavior
🪶 🪶 🪶	🪶	🪶 🪶 🪶 🪶 🪶

Best places to find this species: Blanket Sound and Lowe Sound.

Key Features: Large yellow-orange bill (Caspian Tern will have a more red-orange bill on Andros). Royal Tern will have a white forehead that will fade to black crown on back of head. Hovers, then dives like a missile into the water after fish.Forked tail, white throughout with black head and crest.

Non-breeding Adult: Mostly white forehead, black on back of head.

Notes:

Least Tern
Sternula antillarum
8.5-9.5 in. Plate: 7

Wow-Factor	Rarity	Behavior
🦃 🦃 🦃	🦃 🦃 🦃 🦃	🦃 🦃 🦃 🦃

Best places to find this species: Pigeon Cay and surrounding waters in summer.

Key Features: Small in size, light gray upperwings with black outer primaries. White underparts. Yellow bill with black tip. Yellow feet.

Quick, choppy wing beats when flying low over water.

Winter: White forehead patch is more pronounced, which shrinks the black cap. Black bill.

Breeding: Black cap and white spot on forehead.

Notes:

Caspian Tern
Hydroprogne caspia
21 in. Plate: 7

Wow-Factor	Rarity	Behavior
🖋 🖋 🖋	🖋 🖋 🖋 🖋	🖋 🖋 🖋 🖋 🖋

Best places to find this species: Lowe Sound.

Key Features: Large red-orange bill with dark mark on tip. On Andros Caspian Tern will have streaked head and forehead, differing from the Royal Tern's white forehead and black crown on the back of the head. White throughout, with darker coloration under primaries. Shallow, notched tail.

Hovers, then dives like a missile into the water after fish.

Breeding Adult: Black head and forehead.

Non-breeding Adult: Streaked head and forehead.

Notes:

Bridled Tern

Onychoprion anaethetus

11.5-12.5 in. Plate: 7

Wow-Factor	Rarity	Behavior
🖋 🖋 🖋	🖋 🖋 🖋 🖋 🖋	🖋 🖋 🖋 🖋

Best places to find this species: Inside of the reef in spring and summer.

Key Features: Brown-gray upperparts, forked wings, black cap on head with white forehead and black beak. Black tail. White underparts with black legs. Airy in flight.

Juvenile: Softer brown-gray plumage with a scaly appearance, pale underparts.

Notes:

HERONS & EGRETS

Little Blue Heron
Egretta caerulea
24 in. Plate: 10

Wow-Factor	Rarity	Behavior
🪶🪶🪶🪶	🪶	🪶🪶🪶

Best places to find this species: Mastic Point, Conch Sound, San Andros Airport, Staniard Creek, and Fresh Creek.

Key Features: Blue bill with black tip, light olive-green legs. Slate-blue coloration throughout body. Head is slightly purple with yellow eyes.

Juvenile: White plumage throughout body. Molting juvenile will have a splotchy blue and white plumage.

Notes:

Tricolored Heron
Egretta tricolor
26 in. Plate: 10

Wow-Factor	Rarity	Behavior
🪶🪶🪶🪶🪶	🪶🪶🪶🪶	🪶🪶🪶

Best places to find this species: On the south mangrove in Low Sound and Small Hope Bay mangrove.

Key Features: Blue back and neck, light plumes off the back of the head and rump. Slight yellow around eyes and throat, long bill. White underparts.

In breeding plumage, this bird is strikingly beautiful.

Juvenile: Very similar to adult except rusty brown neck.

Notes:

Snowy Egret
Egretta thula
24 in. Plate: 10

Wow-Factor	Rarity	Behavior
🪶 🪶 🪶 🪶	🪶 🪶 🪶	🪶 🪶 🪶

Best places to find this species: Mangroves near Money Point and Mastic Point pond.

Key Features: Overall white in plumage with black legs and bright yellow feet and lores. Thin, black bill.

Juvenile: Dark legs in front and greenish color on back.

Non-breeding Adult: Lores will be more gray in color.

Notes:

Reddish Egret
Egretta rufescens
30 in. Plate: 10

Wow-Factor	Rarity	Behavior
🪶 🪶 🪶 🪶	🪶 🪶 🪶 🪶	🪶 🪶 🪶 🪶 🪶

Best places to find this species: Staniard Creek flats and mangroves, Blanket Sound at low tide.

Key Features: Besides its wicked dance moves, this bird is easily identified by its bill, in both morphs the Reddish Egret's bill will go from pink-red (at base), to black (at tip).

Dark Morph: Rusty-colored head and neck, blue-gray body and legs. Immature will be slightly duller with an all dark bill.

White Morph: All white with blue-gray legs.

Notes:

Great Blue Heron
Ardea herodias
46 in. Plate: 10

Wow-Factor	Rarity	Behavior
🪶 🪶 🪶	🪶 🪶	🪶 🪶 🪶

Best places to find this species: Fresh Creek by the bridge and Staniard Creek mangroves.

Key Features: Large bodied and long billed, mostly gray-blue coloration. (If you see a GBH lacking black plumes and band on head it may be a WÜRDEMANN'S Heron, so look closely.)

Long legs and neck. Long, spear-like yellow bill. Lighter head with thick black band behind eye extending to black plumes.
Notes:

Great Egret
Ardea alba
39 in. Plate: 10

Wow-Factor	Rarity	Behavior
🪶 🪶 🪶 🪶	🪶	🪶 🪶

Best places to find this species: Road to Red Bays and any standing water.

Key Features: Large white egret, large yellow bill, black legs and feet.

Large white egret, with long yellow bill, and yellow-green lores. Has a forward-leaning pose when feeding.
Notes:

American Bittern
Botaurus lentiginosus
28 in. Plate: 11

Wow-Factor	Rarity	Behavior
🦅 🦅 🦅 🦅 🦅	🦅 🦅 🦅 🦅 🦅*	🦅 🦅 🦅 🦅 🦅

Best places to find this species: Calabash ponds (just north of Calabash Bay).

Key Features: Light-brown neck with streaking. Often hard to see due to its rigid stance with its bill pointed to the sky to blend in with habitat.

This master of camouflage is a smaller, stockier heron. Light brown on back, longer yellowish bill. Dark on top of wings when seen in flight.

*It is probably not this rare, but is so hard to see that it is *rarely seen*.

Notes:

Yellow-Crowned Night-Heron
Nyctanassa violacea
24 in. Plate: 11

Wow-Factor	Rarity	Behavior
🦅 🦅 🦅 🦅	🦅 🦅	🦅 🦅 🦅

Best places to find this species: South mangrove in Lowe Sound behind Forfar Field Station.

Key Features: Pale yellow crown, yellow-green legs. Longer neck and taller posture than BCNH.

Juvenile: Buff brown plumage, yellow eyes, and pale legs and feet.

Adult: Thick bill, black head with pale yellow crown and white cheek patch. Long plumes extending off crown. Blue-gray plumage throughout body. Feathers on back are black with thick blue-gray borders. Orange eyes. Yellow-green legs and feet.

Notes:

Black-crowned Night-Heron
Nycticorax nycticorax
25 in. Plate: 11

Wow-Factor	Rarity	Behavior
🖋 🖋 🖋 🖋 🖋	🖋 🖋 🖋	🖋 🖋 🖋

Best places to find this species: Stafford Creek bridge (hunts there nearly every night).

Key Features: Red eyes. Black crown and back. Dark bill. Yellow legs and feet.

Juvenile: Dark brown back with feathers tipped with white, paler brown below and heavily streaked. Orange eye, top of bill and tip are darker than the yellow bottom. Pale-yellow legs and feet.

Adult: Pale gray upper-wings, rump, and tail. Two or three plumes extending from back of head.

Notes:

Limpkin
Aramus guarauna
26 in. Plate: 11

Wow-Factor	Rarity	Behavior
🖋 🖋 🖋	🖋 🖋 🖋	🖋 🖋 🖋 🖋

Best places to find this species: Near San Andros Airport and fields near Bahamas Agricultural and Marine Research Institute.

Key Features: Large, spotted brown bird with long legs and long slightly curved bill. Has a distinct trumpet-like call.

Notes:

Green Heron
Butorides virescens
18 in. Plate: 11

Wow-Factor	Rarity	Behavior
🪶🪶🪶🪶🪶	🪶🪶	🪶🪶🪶

Best places to find this species: Red Bays (almost always found at the small pond next to Red Bays docks).

Key Features: Distinct glossy green-blue back and deep chestnut neck. Long neck, thick bill. Green-yellow legs. Large body. Very beautiful bird.

Immature: Lighter brown throughout with streaked neck.

Notes:

Cattle Egret
Bubulcus ibis
20 in. Plate: 11

Wow-Factor	Rarity	Behavior
🪶🪶🪶	🪶	🪶🪶🪶🪶

Best places to find this species: San Andros Airport pond and Mennonite Farms.

Key Features: Short and thick yellow bill, stockier than other egrets. Mostly white throughout with pink legs.

Seen on roadsides or in fields with cattle, often riding on the cattle's back.

Breeding: Plumage will show buff orange on top of head, throat, and back.

Notes:

White Ibis
Eudocimus albus
25 in. Plate: 11

Wow-Factor	Rarity	Behavior
✦ ✦ ✦	✦	✦ ✦

Best places to find this species: Very common in yards in Mastic Point.

Key Features: Plumage is white throughout, with longer legs and a decurved long bill. The bill, bare skin on face, and legs are pink or red in color. In flight, wingtips are black.

Juvenile: Head and back are brown in color with white underparts. Bill and legs remain light red or orange in coloration.

Notes:

Roseate Spoonbill
Platalea ajaja
28-34 in. Plate: 12

Wow-Factor	Rarity	Behavior
✦ ✦ ✦ ✦ ✦	✦ ✦ ✦ ✦ ✦	✦ ✦ ✦

Best places to find this species: Very rare but has been seen in Staniard Creek and standing water north of London Creek.

Key Features: Pink body that is lighter in the neck. Long spoon-shaped bill. Featherless, gray-green head. Magenta patch on upper wings. Red irises. Longer, dark-red legs.

Juvenile: White head, paler in color.

Notes:

Greater Flamingo
Phoenicopterus roseus
43-59 in. Plate: 12

Wow-Factor	Rarity	Behavior
🪶 🪶 🪶 🪶 🪶	🪶 🪶 🪶 🪶 🪶	🪶 🪶 🪶

Best places to find this species: West Side National Park.*

Key Features: Light-pink color with red coverts on wings and long bubblegum-pink legs. Signature S-shaped neck and bubblegum-pink beak with black tip. Goose-like honking.

*In 2003 Joe Steensma and Prescott Smith (of Stafford Creek Lodge) conducted an aerial survey looking for nesting Greater Flamingos. A flock of four hundred (estimated) individuals was found just west of Twin Lakes near Middle Bight. Joe Steensma has reported Greater Flamingo in 2006, 2009, 2011, and 2012. It is possible that nesting colonies remain. The best chance to see flamingos is to ask the local fishermen if they have spotted the birds on the west side of the island.

Notes:

PLOVERS

Semipalmated Plover
Charadrius semipalmatus
7.25 in. Plate: 13

Wow-Factor   Rarity   Behavior

Best places to find this species: Joulters, Red Bays mudflat, and Staniard Creek mudflat.

Key Features: Yellow-orange bill with black tip, orange legs. Dark back, white collar and white facial markings. Complete dark breast band.

Immature and winter: Legs are yellow. Band of neck is brown.

Notes:

Piping Plover
Charadrius melodus
7 in. Plate: 13

Wow-Factor   Rarity   Behavior

Best places to find this species: Joulters, Red Bays mudflat, and Staniard Creek mudflat.*

Key Features: In winter bill is black. In spring bill is yellow-orange with black tip.

Similar to *Charadrius semipalmatus* except light gray on upper parts. Single chest band sometimes incomplete. Black forehead and orange legs.

*Our records dating back to 1994 show a slight decline in overall wintering Piping Plover populations in Staniard Creek but an increase on the Red Bays mudflats.

Note: This bird is globally threatened and vulnerable to habitat destruction.

Notes:

Wilson's Plover
Charadrius wilsonia
8 in. Plate: 13

Wow-Factor	Rarity	Behavior
🪶 🪶 🪶	🪶 🪶 🪶	🪶 🪶

Best places to find this species: Joulters, Red Bays mudflat, Staniard Creek mudflat, and Saddleback Cays.

Key Features: Dull pink feet. Heavier black bill and wider neck band than the *Charadius semipalmatus*.

Brown on top and white below. Slightly but noticeably bigger than Semi-palmated plover, piping plover, and snowy plover. Found year round.

Winter: Light brown.

Notes:

Snowy Plover
Charadrius alexandrines
6-6.5 in. Plate: 13

Wow-Factor	Rarity	Behavior
🪶 🪶 🪶	🪶 🪶 🪶	🪶 🪶

Best places to find this species: Joulters, Red Bays mudflat, and Staniard Creek mudflat.

Key Features: Black patches on the side of the chest making it look like a partial breast band. Patches found behind the eyes, on either side of the breast and on the crown. Black, slender, long bill. Black legs. Buff-striped feathers.

Similar to but smaller than *Charadrius melodus*.

Male: Patches are black.

Female: Patches are more gray.

Notes:

Killdeer
Charadrius vociferous
10 in. Plate: 13

Wow-Factor	Rarity	Behavior
🪶 🪶 🪶	🪶 🪶	🪶 🪶 🪶

Best places to find this species: San Andros Airport and the north landfill (dump).

Key Features: Double black breast band. Orange-bronze color on upper part of tail and lower back. Brown on top and white below. Very active at night.

Notes:

Black-Bellied Plover
Pluvialis squatarola
11.5 in. Plate: 14

Wow-Factor	Rarity	Behavior
🪶 🪶 🪶	🪶 🪶	🪶 🪶 🪶

Best places to find this species: Red Bays and Summerset Beach.

Key Features: Black "armpit" in flight. Heavy, dark bill. Largest plover, with a relatively large head. Gray legs. Light stripe beginning in front and above eye towards back of head.

Slightly buff neck and breast. Underparts are white and back-brown with white speckling. Fairly common along beaches and coastal rock communities.

Breeding: Unique black face, neck, and underparts. Sides of neck and around face white. Back is white with dark speckling. White rump.

Juvenile: Pale cap, white belly, defined streaked breast.

Notes:

SANDPIPERS

Solitary Sandpiper
Tringa solitaria
8.5 in. Plate: 15

Wow-Factor	Rarity	Behavior
🪶 🪶	🪶 🪶 🪶	🪶 🪶 🪶

Best places to find this species: The harbor at Mastic Point and rocks by the lighthouse in Fresh Creek.

Key Features: White eye ring. Often holds wings up as if to gain balance when landing. Mid-sized shorebird with moderately long legs and neck. Medium-sized, dark bill. Dull brown back with white underparts. Streaking through back and lighter streaking through chest and head. Green legs.

Notes:

Wilson's Snipe
Gallinago gallinago
10.5-11 in. Plate: 15

Wow-Factor	Rarity	Behavior
🪶 🪶 🪶	🪶 🪶 🪶 🪶 🪶	🪶 🪶

Best places to find this species: Ponds along the road from San Andros Airport to Mastic Point.

Key Features: Long, thick bill and orange tail. Unique zig-zag flight pattern. Interchangeable with Common Snipe. Stout. Brown on top with head and back striped. White belly. Sides heavily barred. Brown rump.

Notes:

Short-billed Dowitcher
Limnodromus griseus
11 in. Plate: 15

Wow-Factor	Rarity	Behavior
🪶 🪶	🪶 🪶 🪶	🪶 🪶

Best places to find this species: Staniard Creek mudflats.

Key Features: Long, dark bill, double its head length. Mid-to-large-sized shorebird. Bill is only slightly smaller than Long-billed Dowitcher. Legs are pale and medium length. Light brown-gray coloration through back. Speckled chest and underparts.

Notes:

Long-billed Dowitcher
Limnodromus scolopaceus
11.5 in. Plate: 15

Wow-Factor	Rarity	Behavior
✎ ✎	✎ ✎ ✎	✎ ✎

Best places to find this species: Staniard Creek mudflats.

Key Features: Long bill, over twice the size of its head. Medium-sized shorebird. Moderately long, pale legs. Gray head and back, lighter underparts with light speckling. Feeds in a rapid, sewing-machine-like motion.

Notes:

Semipalmated Sandpiper
Calidris pusilla
6-6.25 in. Plate: 16

Wow-Factor	Rarity	Behavior
✎ ✎	✎ ✎ ✎	✎ ✎

Best places to find this species: Mudflats at Staniard Creek and Red Bays (south of the dock), and Joulters.

Key Features: Round, short, thick bill that is slightly clubbed at the tip. Black legs, plump, with partially webbed toes.

Winter: No spots on the breast during the winter. Slightly streaked breast. Gray-brown on top.

Breeding: Darker brown on top with heavily streaked chest.

Immature: Strong eyebrow, more uniform color on the top. Not streaked below.

Notes:

Western Sandpiper
Calidris mauri
6.5 in. Plate: 16

Wow-Factor	Rarity	Behavior
🪶 🪶	🪶 🪶 🪶 🪶	🪶 🪶

Best places to find this species: Mudflats at Staniard Creek and Red Bays (south of the dock), Joulters.

Key Features: Black, slightly drooped bill that varies in length. Black legs and partially webbed feet. Brown on the top with a little black. Chestnut on the scapulars, crown, and ear patch. Sides are spotted with chest heavily streaked.

Winter: Gray top with white underparts, light breast streaks, and lighter crown.

Breeding: Arrow shaped spots on the side of the face.

Immature: Eyebrow not as prominent as *Calidus pusilla*. Similar to adult breeding with finer streaks.

Notes:

Least Sandpiper
Calidris minutilla
6 in. Plate: 16

Wow-Factor	Rarity	Behavior
🪶 🪶	🪶 🪶 🪶	🪶 🪶

Best places to find this species: Mudflats at Staniard Creek and Red Bays (south of the dock), Joulters.

Key Features: Yellow-green legs, fine bill with slight droop at tip. Mostly brown-back and buff breast, white underparts. Slight white stripe above eye. Non-breeding plumage is brown-gray.

Notes:

White-rumped Sandpiper
Calidris fuscicollis

7.5 in. Plate: 16

Wow-Factor   Rarity   Behavior
🪶 🪶   🪶 🪶 🪶 🪶   🪶 🪶

Best places to find this species: Mudflats at Staniard Creek and Red Bays (south of the dock), Joulters.

Key Features: Unmarked white rump clearly visible during flight. Long wings extending beyond tail. Black, medium-sized bill; pale reddish at base. White rump noticeable during flight. Gray-brown on top through neck and head, giving a hooded look. Upper-parts are streaked. Whitish below with short, darker streaking extending through flanks.

Notes:

Baird's Sandpiper
Calidris bairdii
7.5 in. Plate: 16

Wow-Factor   Rarity   Behavior
🪶 🪶   🪶 🪶 🪶 🪶   🪶 🪶

Best places to find this species: Mudflats at Staniard Creek and Red Bays (south of the dock), Joulters.

Key Features: Wings extend beyond tail. Brown across the breast and on the top. Straight, thin bill and buff plumage. Green-black legs.

Immature: Back appears scaly because of pale feather edgings.

Notes:

Sanderling
Calidris alba
8 in. Plate: 17

Wow-Factor	Rarity	Behavior
🖋 🖋	🖋 🖋 🖋	🖋 🖋

Best places to find this species: Mudflats at Staniard Creek and Red Bays (south of the dock), Joulters.

Key Features: Runs on wet sand after wave recedes. Pale, light gray on the top and white underneath. Black patch on shoulders. Black legs. Wing stripe noticeable during flight. Lacks a hind toe. Short, straight, and black bill.

Breeding: Rusty brown color on the head, mantle, and breast.

Notes:

Spotted Sandpiper
Actitis macularia
7.5 in. Plate: 17

Wow-Factor	Rarity	Behavior
🖋 🖋	🖋 🖋 🖋	🖋 🖋 🖋 🖋 🖋

Best places to find this species: Conch Sound and the harbor at Mastic Point.

Key Features: Tail "bobs" up and down consistently. Brownish, barred top and greenish legs. "Fluttering" flight and constantly teeters. Shallow, quick wing beats. Round dark spots underneath with dark rump. Legs vary from flesh color to pink.

Immature and winter: Lacks spotting underneath. Brown on top with white underneath. Gray extends from the neck to the breast.

Males: Fewer spots than females.

Notes:

Willet

Catoptrophorus semipalmatus

15 in. Plate: 18

Wow-Factor	Rarity	Behavior
🖊 🖊 🖊	🖊 🖊 🖊	🖊 🖊 🖊

Best places to find this species: Lowe Sound (the prop roots on mangroves south of the main settlement).

Key Features: Thick, long bill. Thick, white wing stripe noticeable in flight. Large, plump bird. Body is very molted black above with a white belly. Bluish legs. Flanks and breast are barred and spotted. Thick, long bill.

Notes:

Greater Yellowlegs

Tringa melanoleuca

13-15 in. Plate: 19

Wow-Factor	Rarity	Behavior
🖊 🖊 🖊 🖊	🖊 🖊 🖊	🖊 🖊 🖊

Best places to find this species: Lowe Sound (the prop roots on mangroves south of the main settlement).

Key Features: Long, yellow-orange legs. Long, upturned bill.

Lots of white at base of tail. Tail is barred finely. Long, slightly upward-turned beak. Streaked throat, plumage, and breast. Barred and spotted belly and sides. Top is brown with black and white markings. "Nods" and "teeters" often.

Notes:

Lesser Yellowlegs
Tringa flavipes
10.5 in. Plate: 19

Wow-Factor	Rarity	Behavior
🪶🪶🪶🪶	🪶🪶🪶	🪶🪶🪶

Best places to find this species: Lowe Sound (the prop roots on mangroves south of the main settlement) and Staniard Creek.

Key Features: Long, bright yellow legs. Mid-sized. Longer neck and bill. Buff-brown coloration on back and head. White underparts, tail, and rump. Distinctly smaller than Greater Yellowlegs, which is obvious when standing close.

Notes:

Ruddy Turnstone
Arenaria interpres
8.5-9 in. Plate: 20

Wow-Factor	Rarity	Behavior
🪶🪶🪶🪶	🪶🪶	🪶🪶🪶

Best places to find this species: Calabash Bay at low tide, rocky shoals in front of Tarpon Pond.

Key Features: Orange-yellow legs, black "bib" on chest. Stout. Posterior upper part alternates between black and white, which is due to an elaborate color pattern on wings and on the rear. Short bill that is slightly turned upwards. Neat behavior: flips rocks with its funky little beak (hence the name "turnstone").

Winter: Brown on top and on chest. "Bib" remains.

Notes:

OYSTERCATCHER / STILT

American Oystercatcher
Haematopus palliates
17.5 in. Plate: 20

Wow-Factor	Rarity	Behavior
𝄢 𝄢 𝄢 𝄢	𝄢 𝄢 𝄢	𝄢 𝄢

Best places to find this species: Money Point at low tide, Calabash Bay.

Key Features: Large red-orange bill. Black head with contrasting white underparts, and brown back. Flesh-colored legs and yellow eye.

Notes:

Black-necked Stilt
Himantopus mexicanus
14 in. Plate: 20

Wow-Factor	Rarity	Behavior
𝄢 𝄢 𝄢 𝄢	𝄢 𝄢 𝄢 𝄢	𝄢 𝄢

Best places to find this species: Calabash ponds.

Key Features: Long, thin, red legs; long and thin bill; contrasting dark back to white underside. Slender neck. Thin, straight bill.

Male: Black above and white below. Rump and tail are light in coloration. Linings of wings are black.

Female and juvenile: Similar to male but brown on the top with paler legs.

Notes:

RAILS

Sora
Porzana Carolina
8.5 in. Plate: 22

Wow-Factor	Rarity	Behavior
🖋 🖋 🖋	🖋 🖋 🖋 🖋 🖋	🖋 🖋 🖋

Best places to find this species: Airport pond and Calabash pond.

Key Features: Short yellow bill surrounded by black face. Blue-gray neck and breast. Brown through top of head and back of neck. Darker brown, slightly buff back with white speckling throughout. Tail often up showing white undertail coverts.

Juvenile: Lacks black face. Bill less yellow with darker tones. Dull buffy neck and breast. Back brown with white speckling.

Notes:

Clapper Rail
Rallus longirostris
14.5 in. Plate: 22

Wow-Factor	Rarity	Behavior
🖋 🖋 🖋	🖋 🖋 🖋 🖋 🖋	🖋 🖋 🖋

Best places to find this species: Pigeon Cays and behind the schoolhouse in Blanket Sound.

Key Features: Long bill and neck, flat body (laterally compressed). Overall brown-gray throughout body; slightly buff coloration below. Light stripe from above eye to bill.

Juvenile: Duller than adult.

Notes:

COOTS, GALLINULES & GREBES

American Coot
Fulica Americana
15.5 in. Plate: 23

Wow-Factor	Rarity	Behavior
🖊 🖊	🖊	🖊 🖊 🖊

Best places to find this species: Any fresh water.

Key Features: White bill with dark rusty stripe near tip, unique lobed toes and large feet Clumsy while walking on land. Dark-gray body with black head. Small, white markings on tail.

Juvenile: Lighter gray on top, pale below. Bill is off-white.

Notes:

Common Moorhen
Gallinula chloropus
14 in. Plate: 23

Wow-Factor	Rarity	Behavior
🖊 🖊 🖊 🖊	🖊 🖊 🖊	🖊 🖊 🖊

Best places to find this species: Tarpon Pond, Calabash ponds, and ponds on the south side of Mastic Point.

Key Features: Bright-red shield on front of the head and bright-red bill with yellow tip. Dark head and neck. Dark-brown back and wings, dark gray under. White stripe on side below wing. White undertail with dark stripe in center.

Juvenile: Bill is dusky yellow. Back and wings are brown with drab gray under.

Non-breeding: Duller throughout compared to breeding adult.

Notes:

Least Grebe
Tachybaptus dominicus
9.5 in. Plate: 23

Wow-Factor	Rarity	Behavior
🖋 🖋 🖋	🖋 🖋 🖋 🖋	🖋 🖋 🖋

Best places to find this species: Calabash pond and Rainbow Blue Hole.

Key Features: Bright-yellow eyes, thin bill, small in size. Smallest grebe. Thin neck. Dark-gray, salty plumage year-round.

Breeding: Black face and bill.

Notes:

Pied-billed Grebe
Podilymbus podiceps
13 in. Plate: 23

Wow-Factor	Rarity	Behavior
🖋 🖋 🖋	🖋 🖋 🖋	🖋 🖋 🖋

Best places to find this species: Ditches on Red Bays road, Mastic Point ponds, and Church's Blue Hole.

Key Features: Dark eyes, short, thick, white bill with black band while breeding. Tawny-brown, drab plumage year-round.

Winter: Lacks dark throat patch and band on bill.

Breeding: Black throat patch. Whitish bill with black band.

Notes:

WATERFOWL

Northern Shoveler
Anas clypeata
19 in. Plate: 25

Wow-Factor	Rarity	Behavior
🖋 🖋 🖋 🖋 🖋	🖋 🖋 🖋 🖋 🖋	🖋 🖋 🖋

Best places to find this species: Calabash ponds, Twin Lakes, and Gobi Lake.

Key Features: Green iridescent head in breeding males, orange feet. Common duck with yellow eyes and orange feet.

Breeding Male: Dark-green and black, iridescent head.

Fall Male: White crescent on face; long, black, flat bill.

Female: Muddy brown, long orange bill.

Notes:

Northern Pintail
Anas acuta
9-11 in. Plate: 25

Wow-Factor	Rarity	Behavior

🖋 🖋 🖋 🖋 🖋   🖋 🖋 🖋 🖋 🖋   🖋 🖋 🖋

Best places to find this species: Twin Lakes and Gobi Lake.

Key Features: Soft gray-brown in color, slender. Gray-brown wings with dark stripes. Fast in flight.

Juvenile: Similar to female, less scalloped, duller speculum.

Male: Long, dark pin-point tail. Dark-brown head and white chest. Gray-brown wings with dark stripes. Black speculum with white border.

Female: Spotty brown, lighter underparts. Brown head and scalloped feathers. Brown speculum with white border.

Notes:

American Wigeon

Anas americana

17-23 in. Plate: 25

Wow-Factor   Rarity   Behavior

🖋 🖋 🖋 🖋 🖋   🖋 🖋 🖋 🖋 🖋   🖋 🖋 🖋

Best places to find this species: Very rare, but has been found at Twin Lakes and occasionally in shallow freshwater ponds along roads.

Key Features: Gray-brown with short, round head and small powder-blue beak.

Breeding male: White cap, dark green mask, white underparts. Wings have white patches. Gray patch behind speculum.

Non-breeding male: Similar to female.

Female: Spotty gray-brown.

Notes:

Blue-winged Teal
Anas discors
15-16 in. Plate: 25

Wow-Factor	Rarity	Behavior
🪶🪶🪶🪶🪶	🪶🪶	🪶🪶🪶

Best places to find this species: Calabash ponds and shallow ponds between San Andros Airport and Mastic Point.

Key Features: Both male and female have a dark bill.

Male: Distinct dark-gray head with a white crescent between eye and base of bill. Light brown with dark speckling throughout body. Black-and-white rear with noticeable white patch. In flight, look for light blue wing patch.

Female: Light brown with darker speckling throughout the entire body. Top of head is darker in coloration with a dark band through the eye and a broken eye ring.

Notes:

Cinnamon Teal
Anas cyanoptera
16 in. Plate: 25

Wow-Factor	Rarity	Behavior

🖊 🖊 🖊 🖊 🖊   🖊 🖊 🖊 🖊 🖊   🖊 🖊 🖊

Best places to find this species: Recorded twice at Gobi Lake.

Key Features: Cinnamon plumage is distinct.

Male: Mostly cinnamon red-brown with brown upper parts and red eyes. Black bill.

Female: Spotty gray-brown and black. Long, spatulate bill.

Juvenile: Similar to female.

Notes:

Green-winged Teal
Anas crecca
14 in. Plate: 25

Wow-Factor   Rarity   Behavior

🖊 🖊 🖊 🖊 🖊   🖊 🖊 🖊 🖊 🖊   🖊 🖊 🖊

Best places to find this species: Calabash pond, Mastic Point ponds, and Gobi Lake.

Key Features: Very small dabbling duck. Both male and female have dark bill.

Male: Distinct red-brown head and thick-green band running back from the eye. Gray throughout body with a white bar on side of breast.

Female: Dark in coloration with blotchy pattern throughout. Featureless for the most part except the light stripe near the tail.

Notes:

Ring-necked Duck
Aythya collaris
17 in. Plate: 26

Wow-Factor	Rarity	Behavior
🪶 🪶 🪶	🪶 🪶 🪶	🪶 🪶 🪶

Best places to find this species: Tarpon Pond and Mastic Point ponds.

Key Features:

Male: White stripe on bill before black tip. White outline on bill when breeding. Faint "collar" at base of neck, contrasting plumage. Resembles male *Aythya affinis*. Back is black. Sides below the wings fade from white breast band to gray through rear.

Female: Dark on back. Sides are brownish with faint pale marking on the sides of the breast. White eye ring. Dark cap. White on face around base of bill.

Notes:

Greater Scaup

Aythya marila

18 in. Plate: 26

Wow-Factor	Rarity	Behavior
🪶 🪶 🪶	🪶 🪶 🪶	🪶 🪶 🪶

Best places to find this species: Tarpon Pond, Mastic Point ponds, and retention ponds where Queen's Highway forms a T going to Lowe Sound and Nicholls Town.

Key Features: Rounded, lower head. Broad-tipped bill. Overall, larger than Lesser Scaup. Larger white wing stripe in flight. Broad-tipped bill.

Male winter: Dark through head and breast, lighter brown from breast back, slightly darker on top.

Breeding: Dark green head and breast. Black-and-white speckling on top to black in rear. White on sides.

Female: Prominent white on face. Dark on back. Lighter brown throughout head, breast and sides.

Notes:

Lesser Scaup
Aythya affinis
17 in. Plate: 26

Wow-Factor	Rarity	Behavior
🪶 🪶 🪶	🪶 🪶 🪶	🪶 🪶 🪶

Best places to find this species: Tarpon Pond.

Key Features: Slight peak on rear of head, narrower bill and slightly smaller than Greater Scaup.

Male winter: Dark through head and breast. Lighter brown from breast back. Slightly darker on top.

Breeding: Dark head and breast. White speckling on top. Black rear. White on sides.

Female: Less white on face and smaller bill than Greater Scaup. Brown from head to grayish brown throughout rest of body.

Notes:

Hooded Merganser
Lophodytes cucullatus
18 in. Plate: 26

Wow-Factor	Rarity	Behavior
🪶 🪶 🪶 🪶 🪶	🪶 🪶 🪶 🪶 🪶	🪶 🪶 🪶

Best places to find this species: San Andros Airport pond.

Key Features: Fan-like crest on head. Long, thin, dark bill.

Male: Black head with white fan-like crest that can be open or closed. White breast with black bars on flank. Black back and burnt sides.

Female: Gray-brown coloration throughout with a darker head, bill, and chest. Buff, fan-like crest on back of head.

Notes:

Red-breasted Merganser
Mergus serrator
23 in. Plate: 26

Wow-Factor	Rarity	Behavior
🪶🪶🪶🪶🪶	🪶🪶🪶🪶🪶	🪶🪶🪶

Best places to find this species: Mouths of creeks, most common in front of Stafford Creek, but still very rare.

Key Features: Green head, double-peaked crest on head. Slim neck and thin bill. Crest on back of head has two peaks.

1st Winter Male: Similar to female, paler gray on back, some green on head.

Adult Male: Green head, white collar, brown breast, gray on side.

Adult Female: Dull ruddy-brown head, gray-brown back, white throat and breast.

Notes:

West Indian Whistling Duck
Dendrocygna arborea
18.5-22 in. Plate: 27

Wow-Factor	Rarity	Behavior
🪶🪶🪶🪶	🪶🪶🪶🪶🪶	🪶🪶🪶

Best places to find this species: AUTEC and San Andros Airport.*

Key Features: Brown upperparts with spotted white and black underparts. Black bill and green-black legs. Dark crown.

Juvenile: Duller in color.

*From 1996-2005 was commonly seen at San Andros Airport but is rarely seen there now. Routine sightings have been occurring at AUTEC. This is a globally threatened bird.

Notes:

White-cheeked Pintail
Anas bahamensis
17 in. Plate: 27

Wow-Factor	Rarity	Behavior
🪶 🪶 🪶 🪶 🪶	🪶 🪶 🪶 🪶 🪶	🪶 🪶

Best places to find this species: Blue Holes National Park, Church's Blue Hole, and Rainbow Blue Hole.

Key Features: This dabbling duck is medium-sized and slender with a noticeable pointed pale tail and red eyes. Brownish in color with dark spots throughout. White cheeks and throat stand out against darker plumage, as well as distinct red mark at base of the bill.

Notes:

Ruddy Duck
Oxyura jamaicensis
15 in. Plate: 27

Wow-Factor	Rarity	Behavior
🪶 🪶 🪶 🪶	🪶 🪶 🪶 🪶	🪶 🪶 🪶 🪶

Best places to find this species: Twin Lakes, the lake due west of Central Andros High School. (GPS coordinates: 24.75566, -77.84474)

Key Features: Blue bill in breeding males. Unique, erect tail in both male and female. Small, compact duck with thick neck.

Winter: Plumage throughout is dusky brown, slightly darker on top.

Breeding: Plumage red-brown from neck throughout upper and lower parts. Blue bill will stand out.

Male: Dark cap and white cheeks.

Female: Mostly dark gray-brown on back, lighter below. Dark streak through white cheeks.

Notes:

RAPTORS

Merlin

Falco columbarius

11-13.5 in. Plate: 31

Wow-Factor	Rarity	Behavior
🪶 🪶 🪶	🪶 🪶 🪶 🪶	🪶 🪶 🪶 🪶

Best places to find this species: Owens Town and Mennonite Farms.

Key Features: Similar to but smaller than *Falco peregrinus*. Tail is strongly barred with white tips. Broader wings and stockier than Kestrels. No facial markings.

Male: Gray or gray-blue on top, white underneath. Tail is barred with black or light gray and has white tips.

Female and juveniles: Brown on the top.

Notes:

Peregrine Falcon
Falco peregrinus
16-22 in. Plate: 31

Wow-Factor	Rarity	Behavior
🖋 🖋 🖋 🖋	🖋 🖋 🖋 🖋	🖋 🖋 🖋 🖋 🖋

Best places to find this species: Owens Town. Seen in flight near Nicholls Town and Conch Sound.

Key Features: The top and crown are mainly black or dark brown with white to off-white underneath. Breast and belly are barred, spotted, or streaked with black. The throat has a broad black streak on side. Wings are long and pointed while faintly barred. Tail is mostly narrow. Black wedge extends below the eye. Wing tips reach the end of the tail and lack bars.

Juvenile: Dark brown on the top and heavily streaked below.

If you are lucky enough to see this bird attack another bird, your mind will be blown. It dives extraordinarily fast.

Notes:

Northern Harrier
Circus cyaneus
18 in. Plate: 31

Wow-Factor	Rarity	Behavior
🖋 🖋 🖋	🖋 🖋 🖋 🖋 🖋	🖋 🖋 🖋 🖋

Best places to find this species: Agricultural fields near Bahamas Agricultural and Marine Research Institute and Mennonite Farms.

Key Features: Long tail with white on rump. Long, slim, rounded wings. May be confused with an owl due to its distinct round facial discs. Yellow legs. Normally glides very close to the ground.

Male: More gray above thanwith black wing tips. White body and under wings.

Female: More brown on back, wings, and top of head. Chest and underparts are lighter brown with streaking.

Notes:

American Kestrel
Falco sparverius
9-12 in. Plate: 31

Wow-Factor	Rarity	Behavior
🖊 🖊 🖊 🖊 🖊	🖊 🖊	🖊 🖊 🖊 🖊

Best places to find this species: Common throughout the island but almost always seen near the athletic fields in Lowe Sound.

Key Features: Rufous coloration on the tail and back, face markings, blue wings in male. Two vertical bars underneath the eye and "whiskers" on either side of the face. False eye-spots on the nape.

Hovers while searching for food. Underparts are spotted black or plain.

Adult: Pale underwings.

Male: Noticeable row of circular white spots on the edge of the training wings. The coverts are blue-gray. It is not barred like the female.

Female: Rufous wings. Barred on the back and tail.

Notes:

Red-tailed Hawk
Buteo jamaicensis
18-24 in. Plate: 33

Wow-Factor	Rarity	Behavior
🪶 🪶 🪶	🪶 🪶 🪶 🪶	🪶 🪶

Best places to find this species: This bird used to be far more common. Increasingly rare. Typically seen soaring, sometimes with Turkey Vultures. Known to be nesting in Owens Town.

Key Features: The tail is short and rounded. Rufous red on top and pink underneath. Dark bars on wings. Large. Thickly built bird with a heavy bill and broad wings and tail. The top of the body is mainly brown. The abdomen is heavily streaked.

Immature: The tail is finely barred on top and is brown instead of red.

Notes:

Turkey Vulture
Cathartes aura
27-32 in. Plate: 33

Wow-Factor	Rarity	Behavior
🪶 🪶	🪶	🪶 🪶 🪶 🪶 🪶

Best places to find this species: Look up! Known as the Bahamas Air Force.

Key Features: Featherless crimson head, wings resemble "V" shape when gliding. **Do not get too close to this bird. Its only defense mechanism is to vomit on you (cool behavior!).** Also poops on its feet to keep itself cool, which is why the legs sometimes look white. Large black bird with featherless legs. Brown legs that are often white from the fact that these birds poop on their legs. Rocks side to side in flight.

Juvenile: Dark head and legs.

Notes:

Osprey
Pandion haliaetus
22-25 in. Plate: 33

Wow-Factor	Rarity	Behavior
𝟜	𝟛	𝟜

Best places to find this species: Nesting sites include cell towers in Stafford Creek and Staniard Creek. Often seen hunting between these two sites.

Key Features: Migrant has a black streak behind the eye. Dark on the top and white below. Dark feathers on the top have white tips. The hind neck and head are white. During flight, the wrists are bent. The wings have black on the wrists and at the tips. Wing beats are slow and deep.

Native birds have more white and are paler than migrants. The black streak is faded or absent.

Juvenile: Plumage is edged with a lighter color.

Female: Lightly spotted with brown on the chest.

Notes:

FOWL-LIKE BIRDS

Northern Bobwhite
Colinus virginanus
9.75 in. Plate: 35

Wow-Factor	Rarity	Behavior
🖋 🖋 🖋	🖋 🖋 🖋 🖋	🖋 🖋 🖋 🖋

Best places to find this species: Owens Town and grassy areas along the main logging road.

Key Features: White neck and face with distinct black marking through eye down side of neck. Short and stocky body. Short bill. Often found in grassy open fields or along side roads. Red-brown throughout back and top of head. Buffy, speckled chest and underparts.

Notes:

PIGEONS AND DOVES

White-crowned Pigeon
Columbia leucocephala
14 in. Plate: 36

Wow-Factor	Rarity	Behavior
🖋 🖋 🖋 🖋	🖋 🖋 🖋	🖋 🖋 🖋

Best places to find this species: Owens Town, Cargill Creek, and Nicholls Town.*

Key Features: White crown and iris, touch of iridescent green on lower neck, red bill with pale tip. Dark gray entirely, with a noticeable white crown. Large pigeon. Can seem loud and "clumsy" when taking off in flight.

Female and immature: Gray or off-white crown and paler than male.

*This species is hunted, and its populations can vary drastically from year to year.

Notes:

Rock Dove
Columbia livia
12.5 in. Plate: 36

Wow-Factor	Rarity	Behavior
🖊 🖊 🖊 🖊	🖊 🖊 🖊	🖊

Best places to find this species: Nicholls Town.

Key Features: White cere at base of bill. Gray-brown. Head and neck are darker than back.

Black band at end of tail. Has a white rump. Black bars on inner wing. Has a variety in its plumage arrangement. During flight, flocks with others.

Notes:

White-winged Dove
Zenaida asiatica
11 in. Plate: 36

Wow-Factor	Rarity	Behavior
🖊 🖊	🖊 🖊 🖊 🖊 🖊	🖊 🖊

Best places to find this species: Mennonite Farms. From 1996 until 2006 this bird was only rarely recorded, but now is routinely recorded in the area of the Mennonite Farms.

Key Features: Blue featherless ring around red eyes. Taupe coloring. Wings are lined with white crescent. Dark patch at base of jaw.

Juvenile: More brown. Brown eyes. Legs are a brighter red.

Male: Iridescence on head.

Notes:

Key West Quail-Dove
Geotrygon chrysie
11-12 in. Plate: 37

Wow-Factor	Rarity	Behavior
🪶🪶🪶🪶🪶	🪶🪶🪶🪶🪶	🪶🪶🪶🪶🪶

Best places to find this species: Owens Town, the west side of Gobi Lake.

Key Features: Stunning bright plumage, white band below eye. A stunningly beautiful dove. Reclusive, difficult to spot and find. Red-brown above and white underneath. Purple-green iridescence on the head, back. Rufous wings and tail. Bill and feet reddish.

Female and immature: Duller than male. Immature has dark border on wing coverts.

Notes:

Eurasian Collared Dove
Streptopelia decaocto
13 in. Plate: 38

Wow-Factor	Rarity	Behavior
🖋 🖋	🖋	🖋

Best places to find this species: Nicholls Town and Fresh Creek.

Key Features: Incomplete black collar on back of neck. Entirely gray-brown body. Slightly round, long tail tipped with gray-white. Often seen on rooftops and wires on Andros. Larger than Mourning Dove.

Notes:

Common Ground Dove
Columbia passerine
6.5-7 in. Plate: 38

Wow-Factor	Rarity	Behavior
🖋 🖋 🖋 🖋	🖋	🖋

Best places to find this species: Found throughout the island; always seen at Forfar Field Station.

Key Features: Rufous underwing, light, scaly head and breast. Small, violet dark spots on wings. From afar, the bird seems plain; through binoculars it is quite a handsome bird. "Bobs" head while walking. Small, gray-brown bird. Tail is rounded and short with black edges and white corners. Pink at the base of bill.

Male: Bluish crown and nape. Pink flush on breast.

Female and immature: Paler than male with brown feather tips on wings.

Notes:

Zenaida Dove
Zenaida aurita
11.5 in. Plate: 38

Wow-Factor	Rarity	Behavior
🪶 🪶 🪶	🪶 🪶 🪶 🪶	🪶 🪶 🪶

Best places to find this species: Mastic Point and San Andros Airport.

Key Features: Red feet. Purple iridescence on hind neck. Similar in size to the Mourning Dove. Brown throughout with black spotting on inner wing. Black coloration on end of wings can be seen in flight. Rounded tail has white tips.

Notes:

Mourning Dove
Zenaida macroura
12 in. Plate: 38

Wow-Factor	Rarity	Behavior
🪶 🪶	🪶 🪶 🪶	🪶 🪶

Best places to find this species: Mastic Point and San Andros Airport. The large mangrove on the south end of the Mastic Point pond is the evening roust for hundreds, if not thousands, of doves.

Key Features: Long, pointed tail bordered in black and white is tapered in flight. Black spots on back. Irregular wing beats.

Gray-brown on top. Paler color on the underside. Sides of lower neck are iridescent purple. Black spots on upper wing. Look at the tail in flight to distinguish from Zenaida Dove.

Female and immature: Duller than male.

Notes:

CUCKOOS AND ANI

Mangrove Cuckoo
Coccyzus minor
15-17 in. Plate: 42

Wow-Factor   Rarity   Behavior

🪶 🪶 🪶   🪶 🪶 🪶 🪶 🪶   🪶 🪶 🪶 🪶

Best places to find this species: Very rare. Recorded in and around Nicholls Town.

Key Features: Black face mask. Buff, rusty-orange underparts. Dusty-brown upperparts. Long tail that is black and white underneath. Bill is black on top and yellow underneath.

Notes:

Great Lizard-Cuckoo
Coccyzus merlini
20 in. Plate: 42

Wow-Factor   Rarity   Behavior

🪶 🪶 🪶 🪶 🪶   🪶 🪶 🪶   🪶 🪶 🪶 🪶 🪶

Best places to find this species: Owens Town, Bahamas Agricultural and Marine Research Institute, and coppice areas in Red Bays.

Key Features: Red skin around eye. Long and sturdy black-and-white striped tail. Long bill curved at the tip. Light on neck and chest. Lighter brown underparts. Light brown on head and back. Often seen in West-Indian Walnut tree feasting on lizards.

Notes:

Smooth-Billed Ani
Crotophaga ani
14.5 in. Plate: 43

Wow-Factor	Rarity	Behavior
🪶 🪶	🪶	🪶 🪶 🪶 🪶 🪶

Best places to find this species: Mastic Point, almost any settlement.

Key Features: Very large, distinguished thick bill; shiny black in color. Look for the sentinel bird sitting on outer branches looking out for danger in order to warn other Ani. Longer tail and shaggy plumage.

Notes:

OWLS

Barn Owl
Tyto alba
16 in. Plate: 43

Wow-Factor	Rarity	Behavior
🪶 🪶 🪶 🪶 🪶	🪶 🪶 🪶 🪶	🪶 🪶 🪶 🪶 🪶

Best places to find this species: Ben's Blue Hole. There's a long-standing roost in the caves adjacent to Ben's Blue Hole. This is private property. The owners are very generous about letting people bird-watch, but always ask. This area is directly east of Coconut Grove. Also can be called in at the dump just north of Stafford Creek and at Owens Town.

Key Features: Round, heart-shaped face. Ghostly coloration. This majestic owl is tough to find. White throughout face and chest with pale coloration on the back. Long legs.

Notes:

Burrowing Owl
Athene cunicularia
9.5 in. Plate: 43

Wow-Factor	Rarity	Behavior
🪶 🪶 🪶	🪶 🪶 🪶	🪶 🪶 🪶 🪶

Best places to find this species: Schoolyard at Stafford Creek. Also spotted at San Andros Airport.

Key Features: White "mustache" on chin. Bobs and bows when agitated. Small owl, long legs, barred and spotted coloration throughout.

Notes:

NIGHTHAWK

Antillean Nighthawk
Chordeiles gundlachii
8.5 in. Plate: 45

Wow-Factor	Rarity	Behavior
🪶 🪶 🪶	🪶 🪶 🪶	🪶 🪶 🪶

Best places to find this species: Schoolyard at Stafford Creek.

Key Features: White wing band. Open mouth in flight to collect insects. Long pointed wings.

Seen mostly at dusk or later. Buff brown and dark brown throughout. White patches on neck, wings, and tail. Most have noticeably white wing band on each side.

Notes:

HUMMINGBIRDS

Cuban Emerald
Chlorostilbon ricordii
4-4.5 in. Plate: 48

Wow-Factor	Rarity	Behavior
🪶 🪶 🪶 🪶 🪶	🪶	🪶 🪶

Best places to find this species: Seen in a number of different habitats, common on the main logging road west of Forfar Field Station. Also common at Owens Town.

Key Features: Iridescent green plumage. Small white "tear drop" behind eye. Small and overall dark green. When seen in good light, this bird's brilliant plumage will explode with iridescent green. Bill is short, black on top and red on bottom with back tip. Undertail feathers are white, and tail is deeply forked.

Notes:

Bahama Woodstar
Calliphlox evelynae
3 in. Plate: 48

Wow-Factor	Rarity	Behavior
🪶 🪶 🪶 🪶 🪶	🪶 🪶 🪶 🪶	🪶 🪶 🪶

Best places to find this species: Look for flowering Bottlebrush plants. Used to be extraordinarily rare, but we have we have noted a marked increase in sightings over the last five years.

Key Features: Stunning magenta-pink throat shield. Relatively small hummingbird with slightly curved bill.

Male: Iridescent green above and white band below. Rufous underparts with greenish coloration on sides. Deeply forked black and rufous-striped tail.

Female: Green above with buffy underparts.

Notes:

KINGFISHERS AND WOODPECKERS

Belted Kingfisher
Ceryle alcyon
13 in. Plate: 50

Wow-Factor	Rarity	Behavior
✦ ✦ ✦ ✦	✦ ✦ ✦	✦ ✦ ✦ ✦

Best places to find this species: Along roadside ponds, Calabash pond, Stafford Creek, and London Creek.

Key Features: Large head and heavy spear-like bill. Unique hovering behavior above water. Blue on head and back with a blue band across the chest. White throat and underparts. Double crest on head.

Will often be heard before seen during flight. Unique hunting behavior; will hover above water before diving straight down.

Female: Additional rusty band on chest.

Notes:

Yellow-bellied Sapsucker
Sphyrapicus varius
8.5 in. Plate: 50

Wow-Factor	Rarity	Behavior
🪶 🪶 🪶 🪶	🪶 🪶 🪶	🪶 🪶 🪶

Best places to find this species: Forfar Field Station and the drugstore across from San Andros Airport.

Key Features: Red patch on forehead, buff-yellow "belly." Unique black-and-white plumage throughout head and back. Large bill.

Male: Red throat patch.

Notes:

Hairy Woodpecker
Picoides villosus
9.25 in. Plate: 50

Wow-Factor	Rarity	Behavior
🪶 🪶 🪶 🪶	🪶 🪶 🪶 🪶	🪶 🪶 🪶

Best places to find this species: Owens Town.

Key Features: Red patch on back of head. Large bill. Black and white throughout: white throat to undertail, white back, black on top of head. Large, distinct bill.

Notes:

TYRANT FLYCATCHERS

Stolid Flycatcher
Myiarchus stolidus
7.5 in. Plate: 52

Wow-Factor   Rarity   Behavior

Best places to find this species: Owens Town and Forfar Field Station.

Key Features: Pale-yellow underparts. Dusty-brown upperparts. Dark wingbars. White throat and breast.

Notes:

La Sagra's Flycatcher
Myiarchus sagrae
7.25 in. Plate: 52

Wow-Factor   Rarity   Behavior

Best places to find this species: Owens Town.

Key Features: Dark "cap" ending just above eye, fading to a lighter gray through eye, continuing on back. Once it catches a bug, it smacks the heck out of it on a stick (cool behavior ... unless you're the bug). White neck and underparts. Darker wings with faint, white wingbars. Slightly rufous outer-wing stripes. Bill longer in comparison to body and completely dark.

Notes:

Western Kingbird
Tyrannus verticalis
8-9.5 in. Plate: 53

Wow-Factor	Rarity	Behavior
🪶 🪶 🪶 🪶	🪶 🪶 🪶	🪶 🪶

Best places to find this species: Cargill Creek on wires (in late spring and summer).

Key Features: Bright-yellow lower underparts. Dark-brown, square wings. Ash-gray upperparts.

Notes:

Loggerhead Kingbird
Tyrannus caudifasciatus
9 in. Plate: 53

Wow-Factor	Rarity	Behavior
🪶 🪶 🪶	🪶 🪶 🪶	🪶 🪶 🪶

Best places to find this species: Owens Town, logging road, and Gobi Lake.

Key Features: Yellowish undertail coverts. Dark-gray head cut off under eye. Light chest and gray back. Gray wings, more brown towards upper wing coverts. Tail is brown.

Notes:

Crescent-eyed Peewee (Cuban Peewee)
Contopus caribaeus

6 in. Plate: 55

Wow-Factor	Rarity	Behavior
🪶🪶🪶	🪶	🪶🪶🪶🪶

Best places to find this species: Fairly common throughout island. Owens Town and Forfar Field Station are locations where you can get quite close to this very photogenic little bird.

Key Features: White crescent behind eye. Also known as the Cuban Peewee. Gray throughout. Will often be seen taking off from branch to feed, then returning to same branch. Will let you get very close for some great pictures!

Notes:

Eastern Phoebe
Sayornis phoebe
7in. Plate: 55

Wow-Factor	Rarity	Behavior
🪶🪶🪶	🪶🪶🪶🪶	🪶🪶🪶🪶

Best places to find this species: Owens Town and Fresh Creek (around Androsia).

Key Features: Lack of wing bars and eye ring. Dark head and back. Always bobs its tail when it lands.

Whitish throat and underparts. Small, all-dark bill.

Notes:

CROWS

Cuban Crow
Corvus nasicus
16-17 in. Plate: 56

Wow-Factor	Rarity	Behavior
✒	✒ ✒ ✒ ✒ ✒	✒ ✒ ✒ ✒

Best places to find this species: Only place recorded is Mastic Point. First sighting was 2014 of a nesting pair.

Key Features: All black. Long, slightly curved beak. Brown-red eyes in front of bare gray patch, which can also be found by the jaw. Can appear to have glossy-indigo plumage in some lighting.

Notes:

SWALLOWS

Tree Swallow
Tachycineta bicolor
5.75 in. Plate: 58

Wow-Factor	Rarity	Behavior
✒ ✒ ✒ ✒	✒ ✒ ✒	✒ ✒ ✒

Best places to find this species: Fresh Creek and road to Red Bays.

Key Features: Shallow "V"-shaped notch in tail. Will often be seen with Bahama swallow. Look for key features to distinguish between species. Deep blue with a green tint on back. White underneath. Graceful in flight.

Notes:

Bahama Swallow
Tachycineta cyaneoviridis
5.75 in. Plate: 58

Wow-Factor   Rarity   Behavior

🪶 🪶 🪶 🪶 🪶   🪶 🪶 🪶 🪶   🪶 🪶 🪶 🪶

Best places to find this species: Road to Red Bays and Fresh Creek. Nesting pair at the pink church in Mastic Point.

Key Features: Deep "V"-shaped notch in tail. Will often be seen with tree swallow, look for key features to distinguish between species. *Iridescent, green-blue on back*, white underneath. Graceful in flight.

Notes:

GNATCATCHER

Blue-grey Gnatcatcher
Polioptila caerula
4.5 in. Plate: 59

Wow-Factor   Rarity   Behavior

🪶 🪶 🪶 🪶   🪶 🪶   🪶 🪶 🪶

Best places to find this species: Owens Town. Very common on logging road by Forfar Field Station.

Key Features: White eye ring. Long tail with inner feathers black and the outer white. Tail is also tilted up, often "twitching" to the sides. Top is blue-gray with off-white bottom.

Male: Black streak from the crown to the forehead.

Female: Duller than males.

Notes:

MOCKINGBIRDS

Gray Catbird
Dumetella carolinensis
9 in. Plate: 60

Wow-Factor	Rarity	Behavior
🪶 🪶 🪶	🪶 🪶	🪶 🪶 🪶 🪶

Best places to find this species: Owens Town and Maiden Hair Coppice.

Key Features: "Mewling" call resembling a cat. Black cap.

Plain, dark-gray color. Flicks long, black tail. The underparts are a lighter gray. Coverts underneath are chestnut in color to a light, brown-red color. Commonly heard.

Notes:

Bahama Mockingbird
Mimus gundlachii
11 in. Plate: 60

Wow-Factor	Rarity	Behavior
🪶 🪶	🪶 🪶 🪶 🪶 🪶	🪶 🪶 🪶 🪶

Best places to find this species: Behring Point.*

Key Features: White tips on most tail feathers. More buff in plumage than Northern.

Underparts are gray-brown with very little white on wings. Streaked on head, neck, and back. Darker and less white than *Mimus polyglottos*.

*The Bahama Mockingbird is increasingly displaced. It is more common in areas where there is not human activity.
Notes:

Northern Mockingbird
Mimus polyglottos
10 in. Plate: 60

Wow-Factor	Rarity	Behavior
🪶🪶🪶	🪶	🪶🪶🪶🪶

Best places to find this species: Found throughout the island.

Key Features: Thin, dark eye-line. Tail flicks side to side. White wing patch noticeable in flight. White bars on tail. Top is mainly gray with a darker gray on the wings and tail. Underneath is white. Wings beat slow enough that they can often be counted.

It is an exceptional mimic. If you hear a call repeated three or more times in quick succession, it is very likely the Northern Mockingbird making a call.
Notes:

THRUSHES

Red-legged Thrush
Turdus pulmbeus
9 in. Plate: 64

Wow-Factor	Rarity	Behavior
🪶🪶🪶🪶🪶	🪶🪶	🪶🪶🪶🪶

Best places to find this species: Owens Town.

Key Features: Red legs, bill, and ring around eye. Black throughout. Will sit perched very still. Not easily spooked. Often heard before seen. It is quite loud in kicking up leaves and debris while foraging.

Notes:

VIREOS

Blue-headed Vireo

Vireo solitaries

5.5 in. Plate: 65

Wow-Factor	Rarity	Behavior
🪶 🪶 🪶 🪶	🪶 🪶 🪶 🪶 🪶	🪶 🪶 🪶 🪶

Best places to find this species: Very rare. Recorded infrequently but most often in mixed vegetative communities. Androsia and Owens Town.

Key Features: Blue head and white spectacles. White throat and breast. Buffy yellow under wings on side. Green back to rump, and white wing bars.

Notes:

Thick-billed Vireo

Turdus pulmbeus

5 in. Plate: 65

Wow-Factor	Rarity	Behavior
🪶 🪶 🪶 🪶	🪶	🪶 🪶 🪶

Best places to find this species: Thickets, Forfar Field Station, and Androsia. Commonly found throughout the island.

Key Features: Contrasting white eye ring and bright yellow lores. Thick bill. It's a noisy little guy.

Adult: Nearly uniform olive in coloration from top of head through back. Overall buffy yellow throughout the chest and underneath. Thick, pale bill and two white wingbars. Dark iris, white eye ring, and yellow patch between eye and bill.
Notes:

Yellow-Throated Vireo
Vireo flavifrons
5.5 in. Plate: 65

Wow-Factor	Rarity	Behavior
🪶🪶🪶🪶🪶	🪶🪶🪶🪶	🪶🪶🪶

Best places to find this species: Owens Town, the road along the coast north from Conch Sound.

Key Features: Yellow spectacles. Bright, yellow throat and white wingbars. Olive on head and back with gray rump.
Notes:

White-Eyed Vireo
Vireo griseus
5 in. Plate: 65

Wow-Factor	Rarity	Behavior
🪶🪶🪶🪶🪶	🪶🪶🪶🪶	🪶🪶🪶

Best places to find this species: Owens Town and Androsia.

Key Features: White eye, yellow "spectacles" from bill to around eye. Two bold, white wingbars. Smaller broad-necked vireo with a relatively long bill, which is slightly hooked. Whitish throat.

Notes:

Red-eyed Vireo
Vireo olivaceus
6 in. Plate: 66

Wow-Factor	Rarity	Behavior
🪶🪶🪶	🪶🪶🪶🪶🪶	🪶🪶🪶

Best places to find this species: Seen very infrequently. Recorded at Androsia, Bahamas Agricultural and Marine Institute, and Owens Town. Often stays high in trees.

Key Features: Red iris. Gray cap. Olive back and rump. Distinct black-bordered eyebrow stripe. White throat and breast.

Immature: Brown.

Notes:

WARBLERS

Black-and-White Warbler
Mniotilta varia
5.25 in. Plate: 67

Wow-Factor	Rarity	Behavior
🪶🪶🪶🪶🪶	🪶🪶🪶	🪶🪶🪶🪶

Best places to find this species: Owens Town, Bahamas Agricultural and Marine Research Institute, Forfar Field Station, and Androsia.

Key Features: "Creeps" on branches and trunks of trees. Streaked with black and white on the top, crown, and sides. Black or gray cheeks. Underneath is white streaked with black. Two white wingbars.

Male: Black throat and cheeks.

Female: White on the chin and throat with gray cheeks. Lacks black cheeks. Grayish streaks. Females are whiter underneath than males.

Notes:

Louisiana Waterthrush
Seiurus motacilla
6 in. Plate: 67

Wow-Factor	Rarity	Behavior
🖊 🖊 🖊	🖊 🖊 🖊 🖊	🖊 🖊 🖊 🖊 🖊

Best places to find this species: Conch Sound, Ben's Blue Hole

Key Features: White stripe above eye. Chocolate brown on back. White breast with brown stripes on breast and sides. Stripes lacking on throat, pale buff on flanks to undertail. Long, sharp bill. Bobs its tail.

Notes:

Northern Waterthrush
Seiurus noveboracensis
Length: 6 in. Plate: 67

Wow-Factor	Rarity	Behavior
🖊 🖊 🖊 🖊 🖊	🖊 🖊 🖊 🖊 🖊	🖊 🖊 🖊 🖊 🖊

Best places to find this species: Conch Sound mangroves and Ben's Blue Hole.

Key Features: Yellowish stripe above eye. Underside stripes run from throat to rear flank. Brown back, whitish to yellow underparts. Throat, breast, and underparts striped.

Notes:

Ovenbird
Seiurus aurocapillus
6 in. Plate: 67

Wow-Factor	Rarity	Behavior
🪶🪶🪶	🪶🪶🪶🪶	🪶🪶

Best places to find this species: Maidenhair Coppice, Forfar Field Station

Key Features: Striped breast, orange crown with brown stripes on either side of crown. Brown back. White underneath with brown stripes. White eye-ring.

Notes:

Prairie Warbler
Setophaga discolor
4.75 in. Plate: 68

Wow-Factor	Rarity	Behavior
🪶🪶🪶🪶	🪶🪶	🪶🪶

Best places to find this species: Owens Town, Red Bays

Key Features: Dark semicircle under eye. Bright-yellow underparts. Long, narrow tail. Dark spot on sides of neck.

Dark streaking patterned underwing with reddish streaking on back. Faint-yellow wingbars. Highly variable plumage. This species and the Magnolia Warbler have more variants of plumages than other species. Pay attention to field marks.
Notes:

Palm Warbler
Setophaga palmarum
5-5.5 in. Plate: 68

Wow-Factor   Rarity   Behavior

🖋 🖋   🖋   🖋 🖋 🖋

Best places to find this species: Ubiquitous
Key Features: *Constantly pumping tail.* "Wags" tail. Bright-yellow undertail with a bright-olive rump. The breast and belly varies with species and seasons.
Winter: Gray-brown on the top with dark streaks. Has a whitish brow. The throat and breast is streaked faintly with brown. Yellow tail converts.
Breeding: Red-brown crown on plumage. Yellow chin and throat.
Eastern breeding: Entire yellow underparts and yellow eyebrow.
Notes:

Yellow-throated Warbler
Setophaga dominica
5.25-5.5 in. Plate: 68

Wow-Factor   Rarity   Behavior

Best places to find this species: Forfar, BAMRI

Key Features: White patches on side of head. Yellow breast and throat. Two white wingbars. Gray back and white belly. Bahamian race yellow extends to abdomen. Migrant forms underparts are white with streaks of black on sides.

Male: Black crown with occasional hints of yellow. bold white brow.

Female: Duller than male with grayer crown and sides streaked with black.

Notes:

Yellow-rumped Warbler
Setophaga coronata
5.5 in. Plate: 68

Wow-Factor	Rarity	Behavior

Best places to find this species: San Andros airport

Key Features: Four yellow patches on rump, crown, and sides of the breast.

Top is gray-brown streaked with black on the back. The colors are duller in the winter than in the summer. Bottom is white with black on chest and or sides. Two off-white wingbars with some off-white, occasionally, on the tail. Four yellow patches on the rump, crown, and on the sides of the breast.

Female: Duller than the male.

Myrtle: White eyebrow and neck (east).

Audubon: Yellow throat (west).

Notes:

Magnolia Warbler
Setophaga magnolia
4.75-5 in. Plate: 69

Wow-Factor	Rarity	Behavior
🪶 🪶 🪶 🪶	🪶 🪶 🪶	🪶

Best places to find this species: Owens, Forfar, Androsia

Key Features: No bobbing of the tail. Whitebanded tail. black-streaked breast.

Winter, fall, and immature: Duller color than males with a gray hue underneath. White eye ring with a faint band of gray across the breast.

Male: Black on the top with a white brow. Completely yellow underneath and on the rump. Underneath the tail is white with black band on tip. Sides and breast are streaked with black. Broad black mask. White patch on wing and two white bars.

Female: Dull-white eye ring with two white wingbars. Duller than male.

Notes:

Cape May Warbler
Setophaga tigrina

5 in. Plate: 69

Wow-Factor	Rarity	Behavior
🪶 🪶 🪶 🪶	🪶 🪶 🪶	🪶

Best places to find this species: Owens, BAMRI, Androsia

Key Features: Dull patch below eye. Two wing bars (one bolder than the other). Dull whitish breast, yellow flanks with light streaking, yellow rump.

Breeding Male: Distinct orange patch below eye. Bright yellow chest and sides. Distinct black streaking on flanks. Two wingbars (one bolder than the other).

Notes:

Black-throated Green Warbler
Setophaga virens
5-5.25 in. Plate: 69

Wow-Factor	Rarity	Behavior
🖋 🖋 🖋 🖋 🖋	🖋 🖋 🖋 🖋	🖋

Best places to find this species: San Andros airport, Maidenhair Coppice, Androsia, BAMRI

Key Features: Bright olive-green back. Two white wingbars. golden yellow cheeks and neck. Wings and tail are black. Sides are streaked. Some white on tail.

Winter: Chin is white.

Male: Chin, throat, and upper portion of the breast black.

Female and immature: Duller than male with a yellow throat and chin. Black on upper breast.

Notes:

Pine Warbler
Setophaga pinus
5.25-5.5 in. Plate: 69

Wow-Factor	Rarity	Behavior
🖋 🖋 🖋 🖋	🖋 🖋 🖋	🖋

Best places to find this species: Owens Town, well established pinyards.

Key Features: Two white wingbars. slight olive streaks on sides. Some white on the tail. Yellow bottom and becomes white at the lower abdomen.

Male: Yellow spectacles. Olive on top with no streaks and white wingbars. Bright-yellow throat and breast with a white belly.

Female: Duller than the male with a faint eye stripe and white tail spots.

Notes:

Hooded Warbler
Setophaga citrina
5 in. Plate: 69

Wow-Factor	Rarity	Behavior
🍂🍂🍂🍂🍂	🍂🍂🍂🍂🍂	🍂🍂

Best places to find this species: BAMRI, Forfar, Jungle Pond

Key Features: Yellow underparts and face. Olive-brown-green back and wings. Underparts are bright pastel yellow.

Juvenile: Same as female.

Male: Black ring (hood) that shapes the yellow face.

Female: Olive green hood.

Notes:

Bahama Yellowthroat
Geothlypis rostrata
6 in. Plate: 71

Wow-Factor   Rarity   Behavior

🖋 🖋 🖋   🖋 🖋 🖋   🖋 🖋 🖋

Best places to find this species: Jungle Pond, Blue Hole across the street from "Love at First Sight"

Key Features: Similar to Common (*Geothlypis trichas*) except yellow extends to abdomen and has a thicker bill with slower activity and actions.

Male: Thicker mask that comes to the sides of the neck with a gray crown.

Female: Grayish wash on head with less, faded yellow on underparts.

Notes:

Common Yellowthroat
Geothlypis trichas
5 in. Plate: 71

Wow-Factor   Rarity   Behavior

🖋 🖋 🖋 🖋   🖋   🖋

Best places to find this species: Near water, low to ground. Very common throughout winter.

Key Features:

Male: Broad black mask with the top bordered by gray-white, while the below is bordered by yellow down to the throat and breast. Dark-olive color on the top portion and yellow below.

Female: No mask with a whitish eye ring.

Notes:

Yellow Warbler
Setophaga petechia
5.5 in. Plate: 72

Wow-Factor	Rarity	Behavior
✦ ✦ ✦ ✦ ✦	✦ ✦ ✦ ✦ ✦*	✦

Best places to find this species: Mastic Pond, Red Bays.

Key Features: Reddish streaks on underbelly of males. Streaking will be light in winter. olive-yellow back.

Stout with an overall yellow body and face. Northern species more green on the top portion. The back, wings, and tail an olive-yellow with yellow wing markings and tail spots. Tail often "bobs." Body sometimes is completely yellow.

Male: Distinct reddish streaks on the underbelly. Top is yellow-green with a crown and golden-yellow bottom.

Female: Duller color than the males.

*Some years it is far more common than others.

Notes:

Northern Parula
Setophaga Americana
4.5 in. Plate: 72

Wow-Factor	Rarity	Behavior
✦ ✦ ✦ ✦ ✦	✦ ✦	✦ ✦

Best places to find this species: Owens Town, Forfar, Androsia, BAMRI

Key Features: Broken eye ring, blue head, yellow-orange breast. Bicolored bill; upper bill is black and lower is yellow.

Male: Blue head and sides of throat, greenish back. Yellow throat and breast with reddish and black bands across front of breast. White belly and undertail. Broken eye ring in front and rear. Two thick, white wingbars.

Female: Similar to male but duller all the way around.

Notes:

American Redstart
Setophaga ruticilla
5.25 in. Plate: 74

Wow-Factor	Rarity	Behavior
🖋🖋🖋🖋🖋	🖋🖋	🖋🖋🖋

Best places to find this species: Forfar, Androsia

Key Features: Bright patches on wings and tail (orange on male, yellow on female). Flitting flight pattern. Very active.

Breeding Male: Black through head, breast, and back. White underparts. Orange patches on wings and tail.

Female: Gray-olive coloration throughout head and back. Lighter breast and under. Yellow patches on wings and tail.

Notes:

Black-throated Blue Warbler
Setophaga caerulescens
5.25 in. Plate: 74

Wow-Factor	Rarity	Behavior
🖋🖋🖋🖋🖋	🖋🖋🖋	🖋🖋🖋

Best places to find this species: Androsia, Forfar, San Andros airport

Key Features: White wing patch at base of primaries.

Male: Extremely patterned. Dark gray-blue above and white below. The chin, face, cheeks, throat, and sides of head and breast are black.

Female: Dark, olive-brown on top and crown with pale brown below. Thin, off-white brow and slight brown cheek patches. Very dull. Smaller wing patch than male.

Notes:

Swainson's Warbler
Limnothlypis swainsonii
5.5 in. Plate: 75

Wow-Factor	Rarity	Behavior
🖊	🖊 🖊 🖊 🖊 🖊	🖊 🖊

Best places to find this species: Owens Town

Key Features: Large, straight bill, reddish cap on head. Brownish coloration throughout. Pale color in face with dark bar through eye. Larger, straight bill. Short, broad tail. Other warblers call Swainson's the "dull one."

Notes:

Worm Eating Warbler
Helmitheros vermivora
5.25 in. Plate: 75

Wow-Factor	Rarity	Behavior
🖊 🖊 🖊 🖊	🖊 🖊 🖊 🖊 🖊	🖊 🖊 🖊 🖊 🖊

Best places to find this species: Forfar, Maidenhair Coppice

Key Features: Dark stripes on head. Dull olive on back. buff head and breast. Distinct dark stripes on head. Long, sharp bill.

Notes:

TANAGERS AND QUITS

Bananaquit
Coereba flaveola
4.5 in. Plate: 80

Wow-Factor	Rarity	Behavior
🪶🪶🪶🪶🪶	🪶	🪶🪶🪶

Best places to find this species: Find flowers. Wait.

Key Features: Decurved bill. Can hang upside down while feeding. White stripe on black head.

White throat and chest. Yellow breast and white under rump. Black back and wings with small white patch on outer wing. Yellow patch on rump. Long, decurved bill.

Juvenile: Duller than adult.

Notes:

Summer Tanager
Piranga rubra
7.75 in. Plate: 80

Wow-Factor	Rarity	Behavior
🪶🪶🪶🪶🪶	🪶🪶🪶🪶🪶	🪶

Best places to find this species: BAMRI

Key Features: Red color in males and yellow in females. Thick, pale bill.

Male: Red throughout with thick, pale bill.

Female: Olive color on back, yellow below. Thick, pale bill.

Notes:

Western Spindalis (Stripe-headed Tanager)
Spindalis zena
6.75 in. Plate: 81

Wow-Factor   Rarity   Behavior

Best places to find this species: BAMRI, Red Bays, Owens Town, very common. Loves Brazilian pepper.

Key Features: Black-and-white striped head. Burnt-orange body. Also known as the Western Spindalis.

Female: Plain gray throughout. White wing patch. Thick tanager bill.

Male: Unique bold plumage. Black-and-white striped head and shoulder patch. Throat and breast are burnt orange. black tail with white bars.

Notes:

ORIOLES

Bahama Oriole
Icterus northropi
8.75 in. Plate: 93

Wow-Factor   Rarity   Behavior

Best places to find this species: BAMRI, San Andros airport, Owens Town

Key Features: Black "hood" connecting to chest and neck. Vibrant, yellow coloration.

Recently added to the Critically Endangered Birds list, this oriole is a must-see bird. Vibrant, yellow coloration throughout back and underparts. Black chest, head, tail, and wings. Sharp bill. Yellow underparts connect at shoulders to back.

Notes:

BLACKBIRDS

Tawny-shouldered Blackbird
Agelaius humeralis
8.75 in. Plate: 86

Wow-Factor	Rarity	Behavior
🖋 🖋 🖋	🖋 🖋 🖋 🖋	🖋

Best places to find this species: Small Hope Bay Lodge

Key Features: "Tawny" or gold patch on upper wing. Very similar to the Red-winged Blackbird, this species is black throughout other than the wing patch.

Notes:

Red-winged Blackbird
Agelaius phoeniceus
8.75 in. Plate: 86

Wow-Factor	Rarity	Behavior
🖋 🖋 🖋 🖋	🖋 🖋 🖋 🖋	🖋

Best places to find this species: Owens Town, Small Hope Bay Lodge, Calabash Ponds.

Key Features: Bright-red wing patch in males.

Male: Black throughout. Red-orange wing patch. In flight, small yellow wing patch is visible.

Female: Spotty brown color throughout. Distinct streaking below. Sharp bill. Light-brown stripe above eye.

Notes:

FINCH LIKE BIRDS

Black-faced Grassquit
Tiaris bicolor
4.5 in. Plate: 87

Wow-Factor	Rarity	Behavior
🖋	🖋	🖋

Best places to find this species: Everywhere, especially when you are trying to find the Painted Bunting. This guy shows up, about the same size and shape as a P-Bizzle, and gets your hopes up, only to see a drab grey bird without much personality.

Key Features: Has several calls that resemble other species, including P-Bizzle. Dark, small bird with short tail.

Male: Black face and breast, everywhere else dark olive green. Black bill.

Female: Very plain. Gray below. Olive gray on back. Bill pale color.

Notes:

House Sparrow
Passer domesticus
5.5-7 in. Plate: 88

Wow-Factor	Rarity	Behavior
🖋 🖋	🖋 🖋 🖋 🖋 🖋	🖋

Best places to find this species: As of 2016, they are only found in Lowe Sound.

Key Features: Stout, striped wings. Brown coloring.

Juvenile: Similar to female, but darker on underparts and lighter on upperparts. Buff feathers. Males have black throats; females have white throats.

Breeding Male: Black, tan, and copper wings. Light-gray underparts. Black mask over eyes and dark gray crown. Soft black patch on throat. Black bill.

Non-breeding Male: Gray bill. Dull, more brown plumage.

Breeding Female: Darker bill.

Non-breeding Female: Buff colored, darker brown on upper parts with deep brown mantle. No crown. Brown-gray bill.

Notes:

Greater Antillean Bullfinch
Loxigilla violacea
8 in. Plate: 90

Wow-Factor	Rarity	Behavior
🖋 🖋 🖋 🖋	🖋 🖋 🖋 🖋	🖋

Best places to find this species: Owens Town

Key Features: Red-orange coloration on throat, undertail coverts, and above eye. Thick, dark bill.

Male: Black throughout.

Female: Considerably lighter than male. Gray throughout.

Notes:

Indigo Bunting
Passerina cyanea
5.5 in. Plate: 90

Wow-Factor   Rarity   Behavior
🖋 🖋 🖋 🖋   🖋 🖋 🖋 🖋 🖋   🖋

Best places to find this species: BAMRI
Key Features: Distinct indigo color.
Nonbreeding Male: Resembles female, with some blue patches.
Male: Very distinct blue (indigo) throughout; darker in wings and tail.
Female: Medium brown throughout. Buffy breast with light streaking. Buffy faint wingbars.
Notes:

Painted Bunting
Passerina ciris
5.5 in. Plate: 90

Wow-Factor   Rarity   Behavior
🖋 🖋 🖋 🖋 🖋   🖋 🖋 🖋 🖋 🖋   🖋

Best places to find this species: BAMRI, Androsia, Behring Point
Key Features: P-Bizzle is an unmistakable species.
Male: This stunning bird is unmistakable, with its brilliant plumage. Bright-blue head with a red eye ring, red body, and green back.

Female: Unfortunately, this female is less bright but still stunning. She has a green-yellow plumage throughout.

Notes:

Grasshopper Sparrow
Ammodramus savannarum
5 in. Plate: 93

Wow-Factor   Rarity   Behavior

 🖊 🖊   🖊 🖊 🖊 🖊 🖊   🖊

Best places to find this species: San Andros airport, BAMRI

Key Features: Short-sharp tail. Pale strip on crown. Buffy-yellow breast. Light eye-ring.

Notes:

Savannah Sparrow
Passerina ciris
5.5 in. Plate: 94

Wow-Factor   Rarity   Behavior

 🖊   🖊 🖊 🖊 🖊 🖊   🖊

Best places to find this species: Owens Town, San Andros airport

Key Features: Flared feathers on crown often give crest like appearance on head.

Medium-sized sparrow with short, notched tail. The bill is thick based, small for a sparrow. Coloration light brown on back. White underparts with dark brown or black streaks throughout. Small, yellow patch in front of eye.

Notes:

ABOUT THE AUTHORS

Dr. Joe Steensma is a professor at Washington University in St. Louis, Missouri. He has been conducting bird surveys on Andros for more than twenty years, but his abnormal addiction to bird-watching started long before that. An owl devouring a squirrel in the winter of 1977 got him hooked and there was no turning back. He continues to conduct bird surveys on Andros and Costa Rica.

Nick Morken was a college student when he was corrupted by Joe Steensma and became addicted to bird-watching. Nick is now a hardcore birdwatcher. After ten years of studying birds on Andros Island, he is hoping to parlay his co-authorship of this book into worldwide fame and "birding glory."

Doc (Larry) Wiedman is professor emeritus of Environmental Science at the University of Saint Francis in Fort Wayne, Indiana. Doc has been teaching courses and conducting research on Andros Island for thirty-five years. After more than twenty years of hanging out with Joe Steensma and proclaiming he is not a birder, he has finally admitted there are times when he thinks birds are pretty neat ... but not as neat as geology.

Luanettee Colebrooke, MS is an environmental scientist from the Bahamas. Her understanding of the ecology of the island was essential to this project. More essential was the fact that she kept the rest of us in line.

www.ingramcontent.com/pod-product-compliance
Lightning Source LLC
Chambersburg PA
CBHW070805280326
41934CB00012B/3064